Running with the Devil

Running with the Devil
The True Story of the ATF's
Infiltration of the Hells Angels

Kerrie Droban

THE LYONS PRESS
Guilford, Connecticut
An imprint of The Globe Pequot Press

To buy books in quantity for corporate use
or incentives, call **(800) 962–0973**
or e-mail **premiums@GlobePequot.com**.

The Lyons Press is an imprint of The Globe Pequot Press.

10 9 8 7 6 5 4 3 2 1

Printed in the United States of America

ISBN 978-1-59921-449-8

Library of Congress Cataloging-in-Publication Data is available on file.

To all those who sacrificed and continue to sacrifice
in the name of law enforcement

* * *

We can't be infiltrated, no cops can get inside on us,
they don't have the resources, the manpower, or the
time to wait. We're unbeatable and untouchable.

—Ralph "Sonny" Barger, Hells Angel

AUTHOR'S NOTE

The experiences of the undercover operatives involved in this book, the anecdotes recounted, and the criminal acts described are reflected in countless covertly recorded conversations, affidavits, interviews and documents generated by law enforcement agencies and the United States Attorney's Office in Phoenix, Arizona.

The reader should understand that for the protection of the agents, it was necessary to be vague in some places of this book, to use pseudonyms to protect identities, and to mask faces in some of the photographs. Although the investigation has now concluded, some of the operatives still work undercover and continue to receive death threats. This book is a tribute to their bravery and sacrifice.

CONTENTS

Contents

FOREWORD

DOING TIME FOR FIGHTING CRIME

"I'm not a worrier. It's just not my thing."

—Jay Dobyns, former undercover ATF operative who
infiltrated the Hells Angels

Jay Dobyns, formerly a deep cover ATF operative, now lives his life as a
public figure whose legacy rivals those of esteemed warriors like retired
FBI special agents Joseph D. Pistone and Lock T. Lau and retired DEA
Special Agent Mike Levin. His sacrifice, like those operatives before him,
was rewarded with threats of retribution, terror, and abandonment by the
very crime syndicate he once infiltrated and by the federal agency he once
proudly served. Dobyns chose to become the one identity he feared the
most: A public figure, a target for the Hells Angels and the Aryan Brotherhood, among other prison gangs, and a symbol of heroism.

For two years, Dobyns posed as a member of the Solo Angeles, a
Mexican renegade motorcycle club, earning the trust and respect of the
vicious Arizona Hells Angels. While immersed in his undercover role,
Dobyns foiled countless death threats and near executions from rogue
Hells Angels who suspected Dobyns was a fraud. He also successfully
thwarted various tests from the Hells Angels, some of which challenged

Dobyns to kill or be killed, ingest dope, and accept women as fringe benefits of club membership.

Dobyns' role in Operation Black Biscuit, a landmark criminal investigation, led to the shocking 2003 bust in which ATF agents arrested fifty people and seized 650 guns, 30,000 rounds of ammunition, and more than 100 explosive items—including grenades and napalm. Dobyns' efforts exposed, for the first time, the treacherous inner workings of the Hells Angels brotherhood and their legacy as a crime syndicate within the United States.

By appearing on national television programs such as CNN's *Anderson Cooper 360°*, National Geographic Channel's *Inside: Outlaw Bikers—Hells Angels*, and the History Channel's *Gangland: Behind Enemy Lines*, less than three months after the release of *Running with the Devil*, Dobyns gave voice to his secretive mission, and became an instrument of change. In characteristic fashion, Dobyns was not one to cower in the wings waiting for his enemy to strike. As a public figure, Dobyns was necessarily protected. After all, the Hells Angels were less likely to target an American hero and risk public retribution for their acts.

Most undercover operatives are destined to finish their careers in silence and cautioned by their government agencies to expect no accolades or special protection. Risk was the life they chose. Sacrifice was the assignment they accepted. But Dobyns, who once successfully infiltrated the Calabrese organized crime family, was no stranger to brutality or sacrifice. Born tough, Dobyns attacked his undercover roles with passion bordering obsession, a zeal he exhibited early on in his career, undeterred by death threats, multiple bullet wounds, and family strife. His whole life was preparation for his final curtain call. Today, he continues to live under a veil of violence, dodging death threats and legal landmines.

Unfortunately, what happened to Dobyns is not an isolated incident. There is a disconnect between what the operatives do in the field and why they make the risky choices they make, and what management expects them to accomplish. Because the operatives are steeped in a nether world for so many months, sometimes years, they have difficulty assimilating back into mainstream America. They have been "institutionalized" in similar fashion to inmates or military personnel who suddenly find themselves thrust into "normal" life, alone with their experiences and nostalgic for the double life they knew and understood.

As a result, some operatives suffer post-traumatic stress disorder as they attempt to cope with "normal" living, others reprise the only roles they know and return to undercover assignments. Still others turn to the public for solace but are often rebuked. They are considered "problem children" and scapegoats for departmental blunders unless, of course, the investigation is a resounding success.

Consequently, undercover operatives are often isolated and alone, choosing to socialize with each other rather than their families or close friends. Some seethe with quiet rage, others endure humiliation as they are shuttled to the back of restaurants and profiled for their likeness to criminals. Many are conflicted by their betrayal of the violent criminals they once befriended.

Giving voice to their experience is cathartic and validates their sacrifice. The hours and hours of boredom punctuated by moments of terror and a lifetime of uncertainty inform the lives of undercover operatives.

Kerrie Droban
April 2008

ACT I
FLYING SOLO

SETTING THE STAGE

THE "WAR EFFORT"—APRIL 2002

Confidential informant "Rudy" was the catalyst for what would eventually become known as Operation Black Biscuit, the Department of Treasury's Bureau of Alcohol, Tobacco, Firearms and Explosives' (ATF) masterful sting planned to infiltrate, and ultimately cripple, the Arizona Hells Angels. The notion of using Rudy, who was a legitimate member of the Tijuana-based Solo Angeles Motorcycle Club (or SAMC), to penetrate the Arizona Hells Angels (HAMC) was the brainchild of Phoenix ATF special agent Joseph Slatalla (aka "Slats" or "Beef").

Brash and irreverent, the large Italian bore an uncanny resemblance to the actor Ray Liotta. Beef was an ATF veteran. His career spanned five years in Detroit and six years in Phoenix. He briefly accepted a promotion to supervisor in Miami but returned to Phoenix one year later, dissatisfied with administration and bored with his paper duties. Beef was restless and passions returned him to the streets and to the vicious Arizona biker subculture he had attempted to explore in 1997 before his transfer to Miami in 2001.

Beef's 1997 investigation focused on the Dirty Dozen Motorcycle Club which, in 1996, had begun its long courtship of the largest outlaw biker gang in the world: the Hells Angels. But Beef's efforts to assemble a task force, code named AMEN, floundered in its own stew of misinformation, petty conflicts, and lack of direction. Interagency politics and jurisdictional issues between the Arizona Attorney General's Office, the

County Attorney, and the United States Attorney for Arizona contributed to the operation's demise. None of the offices would share information or informants with the others and in the end AMEN failed.

The Dirty Dozen were ultimately absorbed by the Hells Angels. And when Beef returned to Phoenix, he had a choice—he could either atrophy behind a desk for the rest of his career while waiting for retirement or he could take a bold risk and revisit the biker subculture. His decision to form *another* task force to infiltrate the Hells Angels was not popular, but Beef did what was right, not what was safe, and although most steered clear of his sardonic wit, they listened when he spoke. Beef's was the voice of experience—no nonsense and practical—borne of nineteen months steeped in the murky underworld of outlaw motorcycle gangs (or OMGs), particularly the Hells Angels and their "junior" club, known as the Red Devils (or RDMC).

Beef knew that the original Solo Angeles were Hispanic outlaw bikers based in Tijuana, Mexico. They had over eighty active members, none of whom resided outside of Mexico and Southern California. Most of the Arizona Hells Angels had never met Solo Angeles club members. Rudy never openly identified himself as a fellow outlaw biker to the Hells Angels. Biker groups were notoriously territorial; the Hells Angels were part of the so-called Big Five that also included the Pagans, Banditos, Outlaws, and Mongols. The Hells Angels, however, preferred to be viewed as "the Big One"—no biker group dared flash its club insignias or "colors" without prior Hells Angels approval.

Each biker group had designated club colors. Solo Angeles colors were orange and black, the colors of Halloween and crushed dirty pumpkins. The Mongols were known as the "Black and White," and the Hells Angels were the "Big Red Machine." The clubs also had their own nicknames, the "Phoenix Hot Headz," the Skull Valley "Graveyard Crew," and the "Mesa Mob" and preferred to be called by their monikers. The *mock* Solo Angeles (i.e., undercover agents *posing* as Solo Angeles bikers) would eventually become known as the "Orange Crush," or more irreverently, "the Pumpkins."

What made Rudy particularly valuable to Beef was his trusted relationship with Robert Johnston Jr. (aka "Mesa Bob" or "Bad Bob"), the president of the Mesa Hells Angels chapter. Most of the bikers were known only by their nicknames—like their club colors, their monikers were a kind of brand that not only revealed their character traits—Bad Bob—but also identified certain skills and titles they possessed. Mesa Bob, as the president of the Mesa Hells Angels chapter, for example, enjoyed territorial rights and did what he could to preserve them.

The Hells Angels welcomed Rudy into their criminal fraternity—the confidential informant, after all, was a fellow outlaw—and supervised countless drug and arms deals between Rudy and members of Hells Angels support groups.

Who better to navigate the gang underworld and deliver intelligence to the Phoenix Group I Field Office than a trusted gangster and ATF informant? Who better to introduce (and deflect suspicion from members of the Hells Angels) additional mock Solo Angeles outlaws to the president of the Mesa Club Hells Angels than Rudy?

The idea was novel.

Law enforcement had previously infiltrated other motorcycle clubs through informant introductions of undercover operatives, who eventually gained membership into the target clubs. Police had also formed their own fake clubs and chapters, claiming to be outlaws in order to gain access to a particular biker underworld. But no group of undercover cops had ever assumed the identity of a *legitimate* outlaw motorcycle club and used that cover to infiltrate the Hells Angels.

Never mind that Beef's proposal to pay Rudy, a doper and multiconvicted felon who had pending federal weapons violations, government monies to deal in methamphetamines and guns in Arizona's criminal biker world was controversial, even risky. It followed Los Angeles ATF special agent John Ciccone's inadvertent enlistment of a killer turned paid operative.

Ciccone's informant, Michael Kramer, had been a Hells Angel for five years before he approached ATF and offered to become a snitch. What Ciccone *didn't* know was that the informant had participated in the brutal beheading of Cynthia Garcia, a biker groupie, following Hells Angels festivities at a Mesa Hells Angel clubhouse. The woman had apparently committed the cardinal sin—disrespecting a Hells Angel—and death was her punishment. Her body was found on Halloween, tossed like discarded trash in a shallow desert wash in Phoenix.

Still, Beef convinced an irritated assistant United States attorney to drop the weapons charges against Rudy because the informant's talents were needed elsewhere. Beef reasoned what better way "to catch a sleazeball except with another sleazeball, right?"

Beef had confidence in Rudy's abilities. So far, the informant had managed to negotiate numerous unmonitored methamphetamine and firearms deals with contacts in Tucson, Phoenix, Mesa, Bullhead City, and Prescott, and with reputed members of the Red Devils, a Hells Angels support group. He had gathered intelligence on the Hells Angels for over a year, identifying more than 140 members and associates, at least 45 of whom were convicted felons who could not even *possess* firearms. All this despite high levels of countersurveillance, pat downs, strip searches, and random house calls to Rudy's residence. If anyone could dupe the Hells Angels, it was Rudy. Short and wiry, the informant's canary grin was disarming and his chatter filled a room like white noise. In another life he might have made a fine car salesman.

The timing could not have been more perfect to launch Beef's plan. Beef sensed brewing tension and distrust between the Red Devils and Rudy. Henry Watkins (aka "Hank"), the six-foot-tall enormous sergeant at arms of the Tucson chapter of the Red Devils Motorcycle Club, was beginning to grumble. Responsible for club security and enforcement, Hank had grown suspicious of Rudy's professed biker affiliation as the only visible member of the Solo Angeles and had launched his own investigation into Rudy's background. Hank had delayed large gun purchases from Rudy until he was satisfied that Rudy was no imposter. Fortunately for the ATF, Rudy's credentials were solid—he *was* a legitimate member of the SAMC.

Meanwhile, Rudy insisted his Mexico connections would aid in the war effort between the Hells Angels and the club's most hated rival, the Mongols. Although the Mongols were another Hispanic-based biker club, they were not allies of the Solo Angeles. Rudy convinced the Hells Angels that it would not only be advantageous to arm his Hispanic brothers against a possible Mongol invasion, but it would also be profitable to establish a collaborative narcotics and weapons smuggling effort between the Solo Angeles and Hells Angels.

Rudy appealed to Hank's weakness: money. Hank made an exception for Rudy even though as a rule he refrained from business negotiations with strangers. It helped that Hank had glimpsed a photograph of Rudy posing proudly with legendary Hells Angels founder and former president of the Oakland chapter, Ralph Hubert "Sonny" Barger Jr., at the Laughlin River Run in Nevada, one of the largest motorcycle gatherings in the country. Rudy was an opportunist and a survivalist. He could make deals happen with aplomb and charm. But even so Rudy was still subjected to strip searches for body wires and his government-issued Ford Falcon was combed regularly for recording devices.

As a result Beef determined that it was too risky to electronically monitor or record all phone conversations, meetings, or transactions, a predicament that would necessitate Beef's use of innovative surveillance techniques and higher risks for the informant.

Beef scanned the array of weapons Rudy had just acquired from his recent firearms transaction with Hank. The guns ranged from SKS semiautomatic assault rifles with flash suppressors and bayonet lugs to customized .12 gauge shotguns with obliterated serial numbers and separate shoulder stocks. "Hank said he could get me fully automatic Mac-10s, Mac-11s, HK-91s, and Uzis, fully automatic machine guns, detonator cords, mercury, and timing switches," Rudy had gushed following a recent debriefing.

Beef didn't doubt it, but he wanted more from his informant's transactions, more than quantities of "glass" (methamphetamine) and illegal guns. He wanted to do more than investigate fringe outlaw motorcycle clubs and gather background intelligence on the Hells Angels and the club's supporters. Beef wanted to get inside the most ruthless and violent of criminal organizations. He wanted to get under their skin, fool them like no one else had, capture their trust and loyalty, and become one of the Hells Angels in order to destroy them.

Rudy was essentially his federal puppet. The informant understood if he slipped up even once, he faced long years in prison—if not death at the hands of the Angels. Law enforcement pressure had chilled the Hells Angels illicit activities. Temporarily. In fact that was the reason Hells Angels Mesa Club's chapter president, Mesa Bob, had referred Rudy to do deals with their support club, the Red Devils. If the deals went sour, the police would target the Red Devils, never suspecting the Hells Angels participation.

But Beef was impatient. He couldn't wait for the big chill.

The hatred between the Mongols and the Hells Angels was palpable and stemmed from a series of events that began in 2001, when members of each club stabbed and shot each other in an American Legion Hall in San Diego. The fight between the two clubs continued several months later in Reno, Nevada, after Hells Angels confronted the Carson City Mongol chapter president at his home for wearing a Nevada membership patch (an embroidered crest) without permission.

In Orange County, at a local swap meet, members of the Hells Angels and Mongols engaged in combat using gas tanks, shock absorbers, and handlebars. The violence between the two groups escalated when the president of the San Jose Mongols was jumped by Hells Angels at an outdoor concert and stabbed. The Mongols were hunting, cornering Hells Angels at bars, and firing at them at random. In 2002 a Mongol vice president found two sticks of dynamite under his cars at his home; the fuses were lit but burned out. In April 2002, at the Laughlin, Nevada, annual River Run motorcycle rally, a fight between the Hells Angels and Mongols left three dead and eleven injured at Harrah's Casino in nearby Las Vegas. As a result Nevada police seized various Hells Angels patches, and the Hells Angels officially declared war against the Mongols.

Patches (aka "rockers" and "colors") represented more than mere affiliation with a biker club, they symbolized an earned lifestyle of hardcore criminal exploits and instant respect and rank among fellow gang members. What distinguished the outlaw motorcycle clubs from more conventional clubs was the three-piece patch and diamond-shaped "one-percenter" designation on their vests—these gangsters represented the 1 percent of the American motorcycle riding population that lived by the credo, "Fuck the World."

The Hells Angels patch consisted of a bottom rocker (an embroidered arch) identifying the territory of the club member (e.g., "Arizona"), a center patch of a figure representing a winged skull (or "death head"), and a top rocker that boasted, "Hells Angels." A full member with all three pieces on his vest was commonly referred to in the motorcycle community as a "full patch."

The pieces of cloth communicated a member's status within the club. Bottom rockers signified a person's lowly "prospect" grade. *Prospects*[1] were probationary club members (one rank above *hang-arounds*, who were merely infatuated with the lifestyle but had no official loyalty to the club), one level below women and dogs, chosen individuals who were sponsored into the club by a full-patched member.

Hang-arounds (aka as "slick backs" because their vests had to be bare) represented the first level of acceptance into the club. Those individuals were afforded less status than prospects and wore "license plates" or tabs around their neck to identify their position in case a brawl occurred and other Hells Angels members were forced to defend their own.

ASSEMBLING THE PLAYERS—TUCSON, SPRING 2002

Beef's proposed plan to infiltrate the Arizona Hells Angels using Rudy's connections met with resistance from ATF brass. It was one thing to send in an informant who was already an outlaw; it was quite another to risk the lives of ATF agents to gather information on the Hells Angels and require that they engage in the club's criminal activities. Beef hardly expected his boss, Special Agent in Charge Virginia O'Brien, to give her immediate approval, but he was hopeful that his countless confidential memoranda to her detailing the potential Title 18 criminal code violations[2] with which he could arrest the bikers would persuade her to change her mind. But O'Brien demanded details: Who? How? How long? and, most importantly, How much was the operation going to cost ATF?

In the weeks of preparation that followed, Beef recruited his cast of characters: Rudy accepted the lead role as the president of the mock "Nomad" Solo Angeles, a persona that not only suited the informant's enormous ego but also facilitated the eventual introductions of his fellow ATF operatives and local law enforcement recruits to the Hells Angels. "Nomads" were full patched members in good standing who were unattached to any particular charter. While they were still required to pay their

---

[1] The terms *prospect* and *sponsor* were sometimes used interchangeably.

[2] Offenses ranged from simple firearms possessions to trafficking and drug-related homicides, RICO infractions, NFA weapons violations, and conspiracy charges.

club dues and perform club activities for the original, or "Mother" chapter, they did not have the requisite number of members (six) to form their *own* charter. Thus, they had to abide by the "Mother" chapter's directives. Nomads typically existed in rural areas where few members resided. They were often sent to these locations by their "Mother" chapter with instructions to recruit other members with the goal of establishing a charter in that area.

The mock Solo Angeles had the perfect cover story—they informed Hells Angels that they were sent by their original "Mother" Solo Angeles' chapter which was based in Tijuana in order to recruit new members and establish a charter in Arizona. Since the only legitimate Solo Angeles members resided in Southern California, the ruse was plausible to the Arizona Hells Angels. Still, the operatives had to be careful not to unwittingly attract scrutiny from the *real* Solo Angeles in Mexico who, despite Rudy's assurances to the team, had never authorized a charter of any kind to be established in Arizona.

And there was the problem with Rudy. Although Rudy *was* a legitimate member of the Tijuana-based Solo Angeles, he had never been the club's president. Rudy's newfound status with the mock Solo Angeles posed some control issues—the informant needed constant reminders, that he was *acting*, that his position as the Nomad club's president was *fake*, that he was really a felon and needed to follow orders from ATF.

Beef assembled special players to monitor the informant, seasoned operatives who could accept the risks of the assignment and assume biker identities with minimal training. Not only did Beef establish a Nomad persona for the mock Solo Angeles, but he also considered various ranks for his puppet club. He needed a variety of willing actors to play full-patched members *and* prospects for authenticity.

It was all theater. It had to be.

Beef was the master of ceremonies, the mastermind, the master.

ATF special agent "Carlos" was a natural choice. Recruited from the Miami Field Division, Carlos was not only fluent in Spanish, but he also had years of deep cover experience working Mexican drug pushers in the Pacific Northwest and Cuban mobsters in Miami.

"How long?" SAC O'Brien's voice drilled in Beef's head.

"Four months tops." Beef was optimistic.

Carlos would assume the role of a newer Solo Angeles Nomad member, a dope dealer who had been ripped off and who needed "Rudy-the-broker's" help to recover his shipment.

"Who else?" O'Brien pressed. Beef recruited two agents from the Phoenix Field Division to play "full-patched" Solo Angeles members. "Who's going to be your whipping boy?" Beef's colleague challenged.

In order to appear legitimate, the mock Solo Angeles needed a prospect. Beef persuaded the Phoenix Police Department to volunteer one of its young detectives—Timmy. Although Timmy had no previous extensive undercover experience, he was enthusiastic, had some knowledge of bikes, was actually a martial arts instructor, and at six feet tall, played a convincing enforcer.

The role of a fake prospect wasn't an easy one to fill. Beef knew that no local cop would willingly subject himself to abuse from a federal agent. Beef hardly wanted to referee the anticipated squabbles between the two groups. He knew the cop would last about ten seconds as a prospect.

Never mind that the traditional prospecting period for a Solo Angeles was ninety days. Ninety days of pure hell and humiliation. Ninety days of scurrying around like a slave filling beer orders, enduring garbage dumps, and generally serving the whims of the mock Solo Angeles. It was a thankless but necessary role and Beef wasn't interested in pacifying egos—he needed to assemble an all-star team. Two minutes, ninety days, who would know the difference?

Beef wasn't about to break it to the cop that the Hells Angels required at least a one year *minimum*, or, more realistically, "as long as it takes."

The bigger issue was riding. Only Timmy and Rudy had ever really ridden a motorcycle. And there wasn't time to teach the others. Beef convinced O'Brien that by leasing an enclosed motorcycle trailer, the agents could fool the Hells Angels into believing that the operatives had actually participated in long bike rides. Short distances posed fewer problems, but Hells Angels were known to ride sometimes hours and days at a stretch in large packs several bikers deep.

The government-issued motorcycles were worn, mechanically deficient, and recycled from other cases. There was always the chance that one

of the bikers would recognize his Harley from a former repossession, but
that was a risk Beef and the others were willing to take. His choices were
few, and he couldn't very well compile a team of bikers without wheels.

Liability was another concern. "What about accidents? Breakdowns?"
Beef pacified O'Brien's worries—the operatives would actually *ride* as little
as possible. Instead, they would transport their bikes inside the government-
issued trailer, unload their motorcycles within one mile of a rally, and fake
the dirt and sweat of a long trip. As Solo Angeles nomads their position in
the pack was at the rear, well behind the Hells Angels. They could go unnoticed for miles. At least that was Beef's hope.

The trailer would prevent most breakdowns, but just in case, each operative was equipped with an emergency tool kit replete with wrench, a
few bolts, and a screwdriver.

"How are you going to pull this off?" another colleague of Beef's quipped.

The plan was simple. The recruits would shadow Rudy for a few days,
practice circling the city on the interstate traveling a slow 45 miles per
hour on their motorcycles, make local bar appearances together as a group,
and, just to get comfortable with each other's nuances, perform small-time
gun and drug buys with the criminal crowd in Apache Junction. Once the
team was visible for a few days and had familiarized themselves with the
culture, Rudy would introduce the operatives to the Hells Angels.

Just like that.

Beef's critics worried that the plan was flawed, even incredulous. *Who
would risk impersonating a biker without mastering the quintessential biker
prop—the motorcycle?* Beef fielded the questions with typical irreverence:
each operative was essentially an actor, and, Beef reasoned, if given the opportunity to play the part of a "real" outlaw, a role that was not only glamorous but potentially career changing, the operative would learn to ride a
motorcycle (or at the very least do a convincing job of *faking* it).

But apart from the issue of motorcycles, Beef reminded the ATF suits
that Rudy already had a connection with the Hells Angels, and the operatives would be adorned in Solo Angeles costumes to lend instant credibility to their roles. Duplicating the patches would be easy. Beef planned to
borrow Rudy's authentic Solo Angeles emblem and recruit the mother of
one retired special agent to sew copies of the patch onto the agents' leather

vests. Beef would also commission the agent's mom to reproduce Solo Angeles pins, prospect rockers, nameplates, and tabs, including popular mottos, FSSF ("Forever Solos, Solos Forever"), FTW ("Fuck the World," an outlaw biker's favorite), Pistoleros de Mexico, IIWII ("It Is What It Is"), and of course, officer tabs to boast each operative's rank in the chapter.

"How are you going to convince O'Brien to allow federal agents to wear outlaw patches?" ATF Special Agent Christopher ("Cricket") Livingston asked Beef one morning over several cups of black coffee at Starbucks. With less than five years on as an agent, Cricket was a former special ops and long reconnaissance team member in the Marine Corp.

"We persuade her that the Hells Angels are parasitic punks," Beef offered, while helping himself to a muffin.

Publicly, Hells Angels members portrayed their "brotherhood" as an eclectic band of middle-aged dough boys who liked to wear sleeveless leather or denim bowling shirts and ride chopped up scooters. Millions of dollars in Hells Angel support gear were sold annually—"Support Your Local 81" hats, "That's Right, Red and White" shirts, "When in Doubt, Knock 'Em Out" stickers, and "We Ain't Havin' Fun Till Someone Dials 911" posters. In reality the Hells Angels were a swarm, a ruthless band of marauding thugs who engaged in drug debt collections, home invasions, stolen vehicle alterations, and strip jobs.

"What about the *real* Solo Angeles? They'll ask questions. It's not as if we can send our guys down to Tijuana for a group hug," Cricket reasoned, pinching the bridge of his nose as if he had a headache.

"We'll send Rudy," Beef said wiping crumbs from the table.

"The distraction that could blow this whole operation," Cricket cautioned, as he dumped the remainder of his coffee in the trash can.

"We'll give him a babysitter," Beef said matter-of-factly.

"Who's the lucky guy?"

"Bird" or "Jay Bird", a nickname the tall, lean and heavily tattooed undercover special operations ATF agent had used since childhood, lived for nine months in a barricaded house on the outskirts of Bullhead City, a seedy desert town across the river from Las Vegas that bordered Arizona and overlooked the glitzy casinos of Nevada. Originally, Bird had been dispatched to Bullhead by ATF to lead Operation Riverside, an investigation into rogue bounty hunters who were engaged in illegal gunrunning.

Bird assumed the identity of a baseball bat-wielding debt collector for select Las Vegas casinos and a gunrunner to Mexico. As Bird's notoriety grew in the months he lived in Bullhead, criminals not only began to negotiate arms deals with Bird but also solicited him to commit murders. The Hells Angels in Bullhead also noticed Bird and began to socialize with him more frequently, often sleeping on the sand bags that lined the interior walls of Bird's four-bedroom cave-like structure. The Angels developed an easy rapport with the undercover cop, making Bird a natural choice to lead Operation Black Biscuit.

It was five o'clock in the morning. Bird's windows were boarded up with plywood planks. His shower smelled of Clorox, a potent reminder of his efforts to disinfect the last addict who had used his stall to puke—not that Bird had many visitors.

Bird's jaw clenched as he peeked between the wooden slats and watched as bomb builder, Tommy, exited his Monte Carlo, with his three-year-old son in tow. Tommy was dressed in a bulletproof vest and motorcycle helmet and was licking an ice-cream cone. Bird met them at the back of his house, the only entrance to the structure, and quickly took the napalm bomb that had been placed in the child's hands.

"I'll be right back," Bird said, as he propped the bomb on the floor, escorted the boy outside, and locked him inside his dad's car. The boy plastered his face against the dirty glass window. Bird swallowed, his mind full of thoughts of his own young son whom he hadn't seen in weeks.

Bird wanted to shove the napalm bomb down Tommy's throat. He wanted to call Child Protective Services and have them whisk away the child he'd secured in the safest place he could find, Tommy's smelly old car, stained with urine and drug residue.

But instead he bit the inside of his cheek, tempered his anger, and negotiated a bomb deal with Tommy. "They're shit," Bird spit, handling the napalm bomb carefully.

"Why do you think I'm eating ice cream?" Tommy grinned as vanilla swirl dribbled down his chin. He patted his bulletproof vest, "I wanted one last pleasure before I blew up."

* * *

"He's mine," ATF Special Agent Greg Cowan answered defensively over the phone as Beef insisted he had better use for Bird's talents. "He's been working Operation Riverside for nine months and we've got enough intel on these bastards to . . ."

"He's established a biker persona in Bullhead City," Beef countered, his voice raising an octave. "He's a natural for this assignment. Besides, the place is crawling with Hells Angels. They'd never suspect he was a cop."

True. Acting wasn't such a stretch for the ex-football player and fifteen-year ATF veteran who had already worked undercover infiltrating the Aryan Brotherhood prison gang and organized crime families. So when Cowan told him Beef had a proposition for him, he wasn't surprised.

Bird rolled his baseball bat down the front of his arms and smiled. He may have been raised in a "Richie Cunningham-like" family, but he could do attitude. If nothing else, he had resilience. Five days after ATF had hired him as a novice agent, he'd taken a bullet in his back (the first of five he would eventually receive during the course of his career with ATF) and bled out during a hostage situation. After doctors fed a garden hose through his chest, sliced open his side, and popped his cartilage with a screwdriver, he was temporarily paralyzed. Not a great condition to be in with a crazed suspect on the loose and armed security guards patrolling the hospital halls. But that wasn't the worst of his situation. No, the worst was his agency's underreaction to the subsequent death threats that Bird received—"Make sure you keep a gun on you and tell your wife to have *heightened* awareness," an ASAC (assistant special agent in charge) advised him.

Interesting. Now Beef and Cowen were fighting over him. Cowen resisted giving up Bird. Operation Riverside was in its zenith; wrapping up the case and issuing indictments now was premature. If Bird transitioned over to Beef's team and joined Operation Black Biscuit, Cowen would lose nine months of hard-earned intelligence gathering. Never mind that Bird would have to explain to the criminals in Bullhead City that he wasn't just a debt collector/hit man for Las Vegas casinos, but in fact a soon to be "bona fide" Solo Angeles biker.

In the end Beef won the match; he recruited Bird to be the mock club's vice president, and, more importantly, Rudy's babysitter. Even better, Bird came as a package deal and brought "Pops," his own trusted confidential informant. Beef cast Pops as one of the prospects. With some bribing, Timmy, the local Phoenix police recruit, agreed to be the other prospect. But Timmy had one requirement, that he be a full-patched Solo Angeles in twelve hours.

THE ORANGE CRUSH

Perched across the street from a local run-down gas station near Flagstaff, Bird waited and watched with a crow's precision as flecks of orange-gold glinted off his jacket in the dry summer heat. His heart beat against his chest like a riot of wings. Dawn cracked against the blue-black sky. He straddled his rickety G bike, anxiety twisting in his gut. Not only was he a shitty rider, but he was also four hours late for his scheduled meeting with Rudy.

"Rudy won't meet us Pumpkins with a bunch of rollers[3] on-site," Timmy had warned Bird earlier that night after their first attempt to meet with the confidential informant and exchange arms was foiled by a cluster of small-town cops who had settled into the gas station for coffee. Task force surveillance had been too slow to move them along. Bird couldn't blame Rudy for ditching his gang of Solo Angeles. After all, the inform-ant needed a cop arrest like a hole in the head.

Beef may have saved Rudy's ass from the federal pen, but Rudy was still the operatives' greatest liability, and unfortunately, right now, their most valuable asset. They needed the reckless son of a bitch to introduce them to the Hells Angels and Rudy knew it, even relished the role reversal.

Sweat beaded on Bird's forehead as he waited for Rudy to appear. Where the hell was he? In less than two hours, his team of mock Solo Angeles

---

[3] Cops.

would make their first public appearance at one of the largest motorcycle rallies in Arizona, "Too Broke for Sturgis,"[4] where they planned to mingle for the first time with the Hells Angels. Bird felt as prepared as a kid on his first day of kindergarten. He needed an Oscar-caliber performance.

So far Bird had only been a fake outlaw for two weeks. He cast a nervous glance at the orange crush of jackets and bandannas surrounding him, his team of mock one-percenters, the only buffer between the Hells Angels and his safety.

Grizzly Pops, the ancient confidential informant who'd been with him for over fifteen years, was a longtime doper and dealer who now made a career out of "playing" one.

Towering Timmy, the Phoenix Police detective, practically begged Beef to let him work with Bird and dirty his hands in the "guts" of police work. Bird studied Timmy's profile thoughtfully. His face was slick with sweat, clumps of beard matted his chin, and a slight tick in his jaw betrayed his nerves.

Carlos was the seasoned ATF agent with just enough salsa in his blood to pull off the role of a Solo Angeles. But even Carlos looked scared as he gripped his recycled bike. And then there was Rudy, president of the non-existent Solo Angeles Nomad chapter and career outlaw biker.

Perpetually late.

Unpredictable.

Dirty patches of heat coiled around Bird, but he didn't dare remove his orange-and-black jacket. He didn't dare betray his fear. Bird slipped his hand into his jacket pocket and fingered his collection of grey rocks— "lucky rocks"—a parting gift from his seven-year old son. "Think of me when you touch them," his son had said in earnest. The rocks were jagged and rough. Bird *did* think of his son and his pretty wife, Barbara,[5] and the fracture of his family and guilt wedged in his throat.

Focus.

---

[4] A rally for those bikers who couldn't make it to the popular bike run in Sturgis, South Dakota.

[5] Pseudonym.

Bird shook off the thought, redirected his anxiety. He'd worked through the night with the rest of his undercover team, rehearsing escape plans, reviewing targets, tightening up backstories, dressing in full gang regalia, and priming his motorcycle. That had been an act too. None of the operatives really knew how to ride. And it didn't help that ATF refused to front funds for new bikes. Registration papers and VIN numbers may have been easier to mask, but recycling undercover motorcycles—even previously crashed bikes—had its risks. Either the operatives would be killed in a motorcycle crash or die at the hands of the Hells Angels.

He revved his engine and glanced at his scuffed boots and dirt-smeared clothes. He may have *looked* the part, but more than image, Bird needed to be sure his story was solid. No gaps. No inconsistencies. No pregnant pauses.

Nerves burned his neck. Adrenaline pumped through his veins. Had he rehearsed enough? "I've been an arms trafficker and debt-collector for fifteen years" he recited. Too long. Bird had almost convinced himself he *was* the ruthless criminal he played. He was a stellar actor. A professional chameleon. Wasn't that the reason Beef had recruited him?

He'd withstood the hammering the night before at headquarters, a tin converted warehouse on Phoenix's south side, affectionately dubbed by the operatives as the Pumpkin Patch. In stifling heat he and his three deep-cover operatives had lined up single file before Beef and a battery of surveillance crew and recited fictitious backstories like method actors. Bird had an old lady in Tucson and two drift kids he sometimes visited.

Fill in the gaps.

Complete the profile.

Know where, why, and how you met your fellow Solo Angeles.

The roar of a motorcycle marked Rudy's arrival. A shock of blond hair blew behind him. He'd picked up a tweaker. Thin, naked legs straddled Rudy's waist. "What the fuck?" Bird stared at the new arrival, his gaze catching the strange skittish eyes of Rudy's female companion.

Rudy flashed him a canary grin and shrugged, "I met Sheila at a Circle-K and thought I'd piss my old lady off."

Bird didn't know whether to kill the informant or applaud him for his brilliance. Rudy's addition at least lent credibility to their operation. They all should have had a "biker bitch" on the back. But Bird doubted his agency would have approved of such an accessory. Excess. Liability.

As if Bird and his crew didn't have enough to worry about, they now had to factor in the female's safety. If their meeting with the Hells Angels soured, they would have to have a plan to extract her first. Damn Rudy.

Hot sun beat down on Bird's face, drained him. He glanced over at Timmy who looked piqued and spent already. "You're not going to pass out on us are you?" Bird teased as he recalled Timmy's earlier bout with heat stroke and food poisoning. Too proud to hurl into dry cactus husks, Timmy had persevered without complaint.

That was more than Bird could say for Carlos who grunted next to him like a rutting goat and complained to him about the hours of overtime he'd invested without pay. Carlos was on borrowed time, loaned out to the team to lay the groundwork for the Hells Angels before heading off to his new assignment in Florida.

It was time.

Bird gave the signal and his team gunned their engines prepared to ride the last few miles to the campground where the rally was to be held. They had already unloaded their bikes from the carry trailer they used to tote their motorcycles as they prepared to make their first appearance as Solo Angeles and mix with the Hells Angels. Not only would the operatives have to convince club members that they were legitimate outlaw bikers, but also that they had ridden for hours in sweltering heat to be a part of Too Broke for Sturgis. Never mind that most of Bird's team knew nothing of repairing or maintaining motorcycles much less riding them.

Nausea roared in Bird's gut. Heat was an enemy they had all underestimated. Sweat and fatigue were real even if the grit and mud on their faces was staged. Because this rally was their first operation and arguably the most risky, dozens of cover team personnel with ballistic vests and long guns concealed under their plain clothing came along for the trip. A helicopter whirred overhead, and a SWAT team was on standby. Bird's anxiety eased as he was reminded that the patches on his back were his admission ticket, instant credibility, and acceptance. Bird and his band of mock Solo Angeles smeared dirt on their cheeks like war paint and prepared to ride into Too Broke for Sturgis like seasoned outlaws. Days of preparation boiled down to mere moments of terror.

"Think of the rally as a mixer," Beef had advised the operatives the night before. "Have a few beers with the Hells Angels, shoot the bull with them, let them see you."

A mixer with enough firepower to blow up a building. Bird counted on Rudy to make the introductions, to convince the Hells Angels that Bird and his gang were strays, loners committed to starting their own Nomad Solo Angeles chapter in Phoenix. Sheila added a stab of authenticity to their image with her brown eyes filled with shadow people. Since she was strung out on drugs, Bird wasn't worried she'd blab or blow their cover. Maybe Rudy was right. Maybe they did need to "accessorize"? It might look suspicious if they rode in with no groupies.

Blend. Mix. Right?

Or risk unnecessary questions from the Hells Angels and other bikers. Unnecessary "sex-drives" with club "mamas." Maybe Bird should have insisted Beef give him a mama of his own?

Maybe Beef knew better.

Female companions might add to tensions at home. Bird had enough questions to field. "How many more times do you want to cheat death?" his wife had challenged him, pressing her thumb into the bullet hole which was still visible on Bird's chest and tracing the prominent "DOA" (dead on arrival) letters Bird had tattooed above the wound.

His wife hadn't appreciated their security transfer to Chicago following Bird's previous undercover ordeal. "You have kids. What am I supposed to tell them?" Her eyes glistened in the growing darkness of their living room the night he broke the news to her that ATF had recruited him to infiltrate the Hells Angels. "It's never been done before like this," he'd gushed, oblivious to his wife's contempt. "Cops have never gotten inside before, not like this, not by assuming the identity of a legitimate outlaw biker gang." He'd continued selfishly until his wife's feral expression stopped him. She could care less about his opportunity; she wanted her husband safe.

She wanted Bird home.

Caged.

Enough.

Bird understood his wife's needs. They were real, profound, and after twenty years of marriage, deeply appreciated. But Bird had priorities and raw talent and besides, as he was fond of repeating to his fellow criminals, "Jesus hates a pussy."[6]

Ouch. Bird winced mentally at his callousness. He'd meant to protect her, not shut her out. Less was more he reasoned when his wife pressed him for details on his impromptu visits home. Bird didn't want to share his dual life with her. Mixing two worlds was dangerous.

"You can't just shut us out and pretend you have no family," she'd protested, hands on her hips, eyes blazed with anger.

"It's not glamorous."

"I'm not looking for stories."

"I *am* a story," Bird had whispered, unsure if his wife heard him. He'd invented his own street theater and cast himself as the lead. He had a bevy of phantom women, convicts, narco-terrorists who called him, wrote to him, worshipped him. Barbara didn't need to know the details.

"The guy's just crazy enough to pull it off," said Beef, pitching Bird's recruitment to his agency. Sun beamed on Bird's face as he snaked the remaining few miles toward the biker rally campground. Wind tickled his goatee and bald cap.

Rudy's bike didn't sound too hot. Bird busied his brain with punishment scenarios if Rudy messed up this meeting. Timmy's face scrunched up as if constipated, and Bird wasn't sure if his friend's expression registered fear or pain, or if Timmy was going to barf again. Only Pops looked ready, his pepper-salt beard brushing against his neck like a scarf. But then he didn't need to "get into character"; he *was* one.

Rudy gave a whoop as they cruised into the hundreds of motorcycles already in the rally campground. Blend. *Right*. Bird and his gang eased in behind Rudy. They were lost in a crowd of chrome and outlaws from various gangs knocking back beers and parading around their trophy women

---

[6] "Jesus Hates a Pussy" or JHAP was a phrase coined by ATF special agent, Chris Bayless, and became the Solo Angeles unofficial motto.

like prized pigs. Adrenaline quickly replaced fatigue. Mix. Beef's order resounded in Bird's head like gunshot. The operatives dismounted, acutely aware that they were "outsiders," chickens among wolves. At any moment they could be devoured. Rudy eventually located the Hells Angels tent where they were met by Hells Angels guards, Dennis Denbesten, (aka Chef Boy Are Dee for his reknowned meth cooking skills) a menacing looking felon who had prior convictions for narcotics and weapons violations, and "Turtle," Chef's porky alter ego.

The two Angels bristled at Rudy's presence. He was known, and feared, among bikers because he was violent and unpredictable. Rudy pacified Chef Boy Are Dee, assured him that his entourage was not there to compete with the club's drug business. The operatives had their *own* lucrative enterprise—trafficking guns out of Arizona to Mexico. Satisfied that the team posed no immediate threat to the Hells Angels criminal exploits, Chef accepted Rudy's statement, "we're guests of Mesa Bob," and arranged for a meeting with the Mesa club's president, Robert Johnston Jr.

In just a few moments of banter Rudy had successfully finessed the Solos' introduction. They were *in*. Just like that. Bird could barely contain his giddy relief. But they still had to meet Mesa Bob.

MIXING IT UP

Two weeks after the operatives' introduction at the "Too Broke for Sturgis" motorcycle rally, the fake Solo Angeles parked their bikes a block away from the Mesa Hells Angel clubhouse on Lebaron Street and nervously reviewed "what if" scenarios, suddenly unsure whether they *should* meet the legendary Robert Johnston. Rudy, relishing his newfound leadership role, taunted the operatives into submission, chastising them for being "pussies," "this is what you came to do isn't it?" Meanwhile, Rudy knew full well that if the team *didn't* make the necessary introduction, the operation was over and *he* was going to jail.

A hot wind whipped Bird's cheeks as minutes later he and his team parked in front of the clubhouse dump that resembled a small prison barracks. White iron security gates encircled the complex and in the blue evening light, the winged skulls of the Hells Angels—"Death Heads"—creaked from the posts. Rudy confidently approached the guards on duty and announced that they were guests of "Mesa Bob."

Ghost, a pasty thin, heavily tattooed Hells Angel, wordlessly escorted the operatives inside the clubhouse to the converted tin shed on the patio that served as the bar where a Hells Angels' prospect delivered cocktails to them. Even as a mere prospect, the biker was armed to the hilt, prepared for freakish gang warfare with a handgun shoved into his waistband, combinations of knives gleaming from his boot cuffs, a collapsible baton, saps, brass knuckles, and a hammer clipped like exotic tools to his belt.

Timmy, who played Bird's prospect, paled in comparison. There were limits to his costume, which unfortunately looked too clean—his newly greased cuts, flushed face, and pissy reaction to Rudy's commands nearly blew their cover.

"Twelve hours," Timmy had drilled before the operatives even started their charade. "Twelve hours of this shit and I'm in."

Bird couldn't blame Timmy for wanting to lose Rudy in the desert; Rudy had played his role a little too well and clearly enjoyed bossing around "Timmy the Cop" with his constant demands for beer, cigarettes, and hot dogs. Too bad Rudy lacked the common sense to know when to shut up and act like the snitch felon he truly was.

Timmy had had enough. He pulled Bird aside, "That motherfucker has me fetching food for him. Fuck this. He fucks with me and I'll beat his ass."

Bird retorted coolly, "You kick the president's ass in front of the Angels and we can pack the tent and leave. Suck it up and choke his bullshit down. Wear your big boy pants today."

"Fuck you. You aren't buying that asshole hot dogs."

"I like mine with an equal amount of ketchup and mustard. Ketchup down one side, mustard down the other," Bird reminded him.

"See if you can get this hot dog thing right," Rudy added. "If you pass the test, I'll bump you up to hamburgers."

Bird thought Timmy might self-combust; his career as Rudy's "hot dog bitch" ended in characteristic fashion with Timmy taking a detour to the toilet to spread Rudy's dog with extra "secret sauce." Not surprisingly, less than twenty-four hours later, Timmy had snatched a spare Solo Angeles patch from the ATF evidence locker and commissioned his wife to sew it on his vest at three o'clock in the morning.

The clubhouse was fairly quiet, considering it was nearly nine o'clock in the evening. The place reeked of sweat, beer, stale sex, and marijuana and resembled a run-down fraternity house. The walls were splashed with red and white, the Hells Angels colors, and eerily reminded Bird of a checkerboard. Plaques lined the walls commemorating the "achievements" of various members; a large mural of a winged skull covered in graffiti on the back wall—member names scribbled in crayon, ink, and pencil.

Mesa Bob appeared in the milky darkness, a six foot five burly biker dripping with gold chains reminiscent of a Mafia godfather. He greeted the operatives with a warm handshake as if he had known them a long time or at least approved of their reputation. Rudy had paved sufficient road for at least a preliminary level of trust between the bikers.

"You are my personal guests," the president breezed with the ease of a used car salesman (which was what he was in his day job) and slapped a Mesa support sticker in Bird's hand, "put it on your motorcycle."

The chapter president motioned for Bird and the others to take a seat. The bar resembled a lounge, overcrowded with beater couches. Bird hugged the edge of a cushion as the president sank across from him, steepled his fingers on the table, and affirmed, "You have my permission to traffic narcotics in Arizona with club support." Then with a hint of mischief in his eye, he nodded toward the back bedroom, "Too bad you missed last night's entertainment. A group of airline stewardesses treated us to a sex orgy."

Marijuana smoke hung like gauze over the bar. Voices filtered in and out of earshot filling the space with white noise, a cluster of Hells Angels full-patched club "Enforcers" huddled nearby, ready to put a bullet through Bird's head if he looked at them sideways. Bird didn't flinch. He sensed these clowns could smell fear like a predator smells fear from a cornered buck in a wooded clearing. Thankfully, Rudy was in his element, chattering away with Mesa Bob about the Mongols situation and dropping hints that "his boys" had business in Bullhead. Timmy was dutifully filling beer steins, and Pops was staving off regular offers of hits of methamphetamine.

Bird watched Rudy nervously as he swilled almost an entire pitcher of beer and snapped his fingers at Timmy to get him another. Just what Bird needed, a *drunk* informant to control. After an hour and a half of tension, Bob suggested they move the party to the Spirits Lounge in Gilbert. But first, he offered them each a "road bump" from the stash of methamphetamine he hid in a back room in the clubhouse.

Bird flashed Rudy a warning, "Don't you fuck this up," he telegraphed, already plotting in his head ways to eliminate the informant. Timmy visibly tensed and Bird made a mental note to chastise him when they had a private moment. Only Pops and Carlos played it cool, shrugging off the invitation as premature; they were already buzzed and the last thing they needed was more reason to attract the cops. Bird knew it was just a matter of time before the Pumpkins would have to dodge dope again. The Hells Angels offered up glass like candy, considering it "a fringe benefit of membership." The operatives needed a collective plan, something well rehearsed and calculated, preferable to being speared by the large fourteen-inch butcher knife Johnston wore on his side.

It was nearly midnight when Bird and the others arrived at the Spirits Lounge. Bird should have been exhausted, but adrenaline pumped through his veins like speed. The place rocked with heavy metal tunes so loud Bird felt his chest compress. Inside, members of the Lost Dutchman Motorcycle Club hugged the corners. Hells Angel members escorted Bird and his flock to a private section of the bar, while Timmy and Pops frenetically guarded the Solos' motorcycles and deflected Ghost's offers of narcotics. Ghost quickly tired of toying with the prospects and returned to Mesa Bob's table where he made it a point to remove his ballistic vest. "We're required to wear these in public, but I'm the only member who follows club protocol," Ghost scowled, handing his vest to Timmy to deliver to a Hells Angel prospect in the parking lot.

Meanwhile, a tweaker approached their table, wisps of blond hair teased the waif's forehead, small narcotic blisters bubbled at the sides of her mouth, and her eyes sank into tight flesh. Her pale blue T-shirt screamed, "The Bitch Is Back." The ghostlike woman slid onto Bird's lap, wrapped her paper-thin arms around his neck, and nibbled his left ear. No one seemed to notice. Bikers wore women like cheap jewelry. Property, objects to be used, abused, auctioned for pennies, and *shared*. If Bird resisted the woman's advances, alarms would sound—after all, who wouldn't want an easy fuck?

Ghost's eyes skimmed over Bird, testing him, baiting him—would he, wouldn't he—but after a tense moment, Ghost spit at the bitch and barked, "Beat it." They had important business to discuss, the brewing tension in Mexico between the Hells Angels and Mongols required immediate attention. Unflinching, the woman licked Bird's ear and whispered, "Later."

"I need a woman," Bird had argued during a briefing at operation headquarters, otherwise known as "the Pumpkin Patch" and "Black Biscuit Kangaroo Court."

"Don't we all?" Beef had countered as he cleaned the lizard cage.

"Sooner or later, they're going to wonder why my old lady doesn't come around," Bird had protested, but Beef pointed with his middle finger to the plaque mounted on the wall in the warehouse: Beef's Rules: No Bitching. No Whining. Translation: He was working on the problem. Trouble was there weren't too many prospects. The only available women were either too seasoned or too butch to blend as biker chicks, or they were simply too skittish and likely to get Bird killed. Still, Bird could only stave off the female bait for so long before he attracted suspicion.

At one o'clock in the morning, Bird and the others returned to the Mesa clubhouse for more beer and conversation. Edge replaced fatigue. Bird heard nothing but sounds—barks of laughter, half sentences, and sucking sweaty bodies coupling on green plastic chairs next to him. Dawn was his relief, his ticket to mount his motorcycle and haul his sorry ass back to the Pumpkin Patch for his nightly debriefing. He took small comfort in the notion that his arrival would signal reprieve for his cover team, surveillance personnel that geared up for nights of gambling and cyberporn watching on their laptops. Scorched patches of highway stretched ahead of him, tempted him to turn his bike home, just for a moment, to check in on his pretty wife . . . Bird had no family. Not tonight.

Memory was such sickness.

Tonight, he'd take winding back roads to the warehouse and avoid potential tails. He'd eventually lie down alongside the mock Solos, on a dirty stained cot in a barricaded house in South Phoenix, too hyped to sleep.

HOME SWEET HOME

Black Biscuit's "headquarters" was an inconspicuous warehouse, a swelter-ing tin box with no windows, a commercial office space, and garage shoved into a dirty pocket of street on Tempe's south side. Beef had waded through significant bureaucratic sludge to establish a convincing "business front." The space was large enough to store undercover vehicles and in-vestigative equipment short-term. Securing a place to conduct operations was no small feat given Beef's limitations—his team was too large and the security issues too risky to meet at the Phoenix Field Division office. Beef needed a place to debrief and coordinate undercover and surveillance op-erations, but more importantly he needed to maintain and secure the in-tegrity of the operatives.

Beef had obtained ASAC Joe Gordon's approval and funding to lease a commercial plot, pay all of the utilities, install multiple phone lines, and obtain backstopped undercover identifications. But setting up at head-quarters was only half the battle. Beef also had to contend with Gordon's predictable threats: "I could shut this operation down any time I want." In fact Gordon needn't have bothered with words. He had already jeop-ardized the entire operation just by appearing at Black Biscuit's off-site unannounced for "emergency meetings" dressed in his ATF polo shirt and dribbling Egg McMuffin from his chin. Gordon's profound ignorance marked the difference between suits and street agents for whom survival was more than just an intellectual exercise.

Beef perpetuated the theater. He created business cards that advertised in bold gold print, "Black Biscuit Enterprises." The name derived from hockey, another blood sport. Beef planned for the operatives to infiltrate the Hells Angels with the speed and precision of a well-aimed hockey puck—a "black biscuit." Beef provided the agents with credit cards in fictitious identities, fake credit histories, and fake insurance.

"It's all about allowing criminals to form an inaccurate conclusion from accurate observations," Bird repeated often to his crew. "It's what's inside that helps you survive." They all *looked* the part of outlaw bikers, particularly after they'd soiled their cuts in grease, dirt, and beer; scarred the leather with knife scrapes; and ran a truck and trailer over the threads to give the vests that "never been washed before" biker look. Poor hygiene, skinned heads, scraggly beards, and tattooed arms completed the bad boy image.

Much to the protests of their wives.

"I'd like one day to be seated in the *front* of a restaurant," Bird's wife had lamented to him on one rare occasion he'd actually attempted a date.

She should have been used to Bird's persona as a "street agent" after twenty years of marriage; she knew he was no pencil-neck and never would be. Still, Bird suspected she'd never really accepted the sacrifice that came with undercover work, the single-minded focus, the sleep deprivation, the strange isolation that only those in deep cover lived, the duality that perhaps only great actors understood. He knew why Beef had chosen him for this role . . . because there was no one else.

Ego had nothing to do with it; practicality dictated Beef's decision. Beef needed someone on the *inside*, someone he could trust, who already had a formed identity, who blended with a murky bastard pack of outlaws, and who so completely lived his role that he would never compromise the investigation. Bird had already had five confirmed death threats against him in his ATF career, and rather than cower or relocate, he had accepted ATF's "condolences": members of ATF's Special Response Team armed with assault rifles had camped out in his home, tailed his children around as they drove their Tonka Trucks into sand ditches, and grilled florists who showed up at his front door to deliver white carnations from concerned neighbors and friends.

Beef must have sensed that Bird wasn't cut out for "the chicken circuit," the fame and notoriety that sometimes came with great undercover performances. Bird's gift was street smarts, and as much as the bureau liked to believe it actually "trained" its undercover agents, Bird instinctively lived the rules—create a convincing background, know the parameters of what can and cannot be done legally, understand when to get out of a bad situation, know the difference between entrapment and *investigation*, and never partake in drug use. There were always exceptions of course. Bird knew that if he perceived his life to be in grave danger, he could ingest an illegal substance and the bureau would probably exonerate him. But the follow-up paperwork alone was enough to deter him from ever testing that exception.

Bird understood his mission. It wasn't enough for ATF to infiltrate the Arizona Hells Angels and cripple their organization. ATF also had to ensure that the risks of the operation paid off in indictments and criminal prosecutions. It wasn't uncommon for outlaw biker gang members to put out contract hits on federal prosecutors and agents alike, eliminate material witnesses, and murder informants before trial. Much like a terrorist organization, the gangs ruled by fear, orchestrating a network of criminal masterminds whose mission it was to disrupt and chill investigations into club activities. They were *organized* killers. Their clubs were run like corporations, with bylaws and constitutions, protocol and rank and file. Even if Bird was successful in bringing down the Hells Angels, he still had to contend with the judges and jurors who might eventually be bought to acquit.

TIJUANA

Word spread fast in the biker community that the Solo Angeles were in Arizona as Mesa Bob's guests and had full-patched members in Bullhead City. Still, Bird was careful to follow Hells Angel protocol and Mesa Bob's specific instructions that Bird seek permission to wear his Solo cuts in Bullhead from Hells Angel senior Arizona nomad member, Donald Smith, aka "Smitty," a hefty mechanic who reputedly ruled Bullhead City and enjoyed a special rapport with law enforcement.

The decision to meet with Smitty was more strategic than practical, particularly if Bird didn't want a bullet in his back. Smitty didn't appreciate challenges to his leadership. Bird had previously met Smitty when he played the role of the local gun runner; now Bird would have to explain why he'd deceived and lied to Smitty and the very criminals who had befriended him for nine months, not telling them that he was in fact an outlaw biker.

"Ask Smitty why I'm out of the club," Dave B., an ex-Hells Angel, said to Bird one evening at O'Leary's Bar in Bullhead City after helping himself to Bird's pitcher of beer. Dave was a stocky character with a red, sweaty face that resembled a blowtorch. He turned over his hand to show Bird his Death Head tattoo; the ink displayed an "out date," signifying that Dave had "expired." He had apparently challenged Smitty's leadership. Later, Smitty would confide to Bird that Dave had died of "natural causes," but not after first relinquishing the title of his motorcycle to Smitty for "safe keeping."

Bird and Carlos met Smitty for dinner in Smitty's sanctum, a seedy bar called the Inferno. Smitty brought his pixyish wife, Lydia, and fellow Hells Angel member Chef Boy Are Dee. Satisfied that the Solos had Mesa Bob's blessing to thrive in Bullhead City, Smitty gave Bird the okay to fly his colors but admonished the Solos that "he does not like death unless he is the cause of it."

Note taken. Remarkably, within a few weeks of operating, the Solo Angeles had obtained the blessing of two Hells Angels leaders to operate openly in the state.

A show of gratitude might be in order. At Bird's instruction Rudy extended a "thank you" to the Mesa Hells Angels on behalf of the Solos, a large cash donation of $500 for their "defense" fund. It was a gesture that would later prove to be critical for the operatives in earning the trust of the Angels. Deference was the first sign of respect. With any luck such bribery might work to pacify the *real* Solo Angeles in Mexico who had started to grumble about the nomad presence in Bullhead City. The operatives learned over waffles one morning that Rudy had, not surprisingly, failed to obtain permission from the mother chapter in Tijuana for the Solos to fly the Nomad insignia in Arizona.

Bird, Carlos, and Rudy immediately arranged a meeting with "Teacher," a senior member of the Solo Angeles, at his Sylmar, California, home. After two hours of explanation and insincere apology for invading Solo turf without permission, "Teacher" insisted that the new nomad members make good on their delinquent club dues and travel to Tijuana, Mexico, to meet with the club's international president, "Suzuki."

"No fucking way," Beef slammed his fist down on the table.

"We have no choice," Bird insisted.

"I'm not sending federal agents across the border posing as outlaw bikers," Beef steamed, his head spinning with the logistical, safety, and legal ramifications of such a venture. It was difficult enough to assemble surveillance teams in Arizona to assist the operatives and ensure that they remained unharmed, but to organize such a task force on foreign turf begged for trouble. He wasn't about to lose control of the mission or risk exposing the operatives outside the country. If anything happened in Mexico, if the Solos suspected the operatives were frauds, Beef would have his hands full trying to extricate his team to safety, let alone explain to brass the murder of a federal agent.

"You won't have to," Bird pacified him. "We'll send Rudy and Pops."

Pops wasn't an ideal choice considering that out of the 170 members of the Solos only 5 of them were white. But their options were limited and risky. Pops and Rudy couldn't be monitored south of the border. Control was key with informants; there was no such thing as trust. Beef was about to break that cardinal rule and he could barely stand it. ASAC Gordon's thundering voice resounded in his head like buckshot: "I could shut this operation down anytime I want."

"You fuck this up and you can kiss the inside of a prison urinal," Beef warned Rudy as he made the arrangements. As if the informant needed reminders, much less responsibility.

"Don't you even think about going with them." Beef wagged a finger at Bird, a mixture of panic and sheer desperation in his eyes. Bird knew better than to protest, still, for a fleeting insane moment, he contemplated the unthinkable . . . who would know if he slipped across the border? Beef knew Bird too well, knew Bird was just daring enough to risk an excursion to Mexico. And why not? If Bird was willing to pretend to ride a motorcycle, he could certainly fake a convincing introduction to the real Solo Angeles.

Pops and Rudy arrived late afternoon to the Solo Angeles clubhouse in Tijuana. The quarters resembled a large outhouse and smelled just as pretty. No one was inside except Suzuki, a spidery figure with a shock of black hair, a too-large head, and small bitten eyes that registered the informants as if they were prey. Not a word was uttered. Moments passed and soon other Solo Angeles members arrived, pumped for their "church" meeting, and at least curious to have new members present. This was going to be a big night—members of the Top Hatters Motorcycle Club were expected to be patched over as Solos. Not everyone was pleased to see the informants; they were outsiders and woefully behind in their club dues. Church was just a club euphemism for official meeting. Like any club, members were expected to pay dues, attend gatherings, and further club business. The organization had bylaws and a constitution and a hierarchy that was more learned than earned. The "sermon" was conducted in Spanish, and Pops didn't understand a word.

Afterward, Suzuki ordered Rudy to pay an $800 fee to start an Arizona nomad chapter and a fine for his three-year absence from the club. But if the nomad chapter really wanted Suzuki's blessing, Rudy would have to cough up a Harley Davison Evolution Sportster motorcycle and they'd call it even. But that wasn't the worst of it. Pops cringed when Suzuki informed them that they were expected to send a representative monthly to Tijuana to attend church and to bring money.

"We're not giving him a fucking motorcycle."

Beef was adamant.

RUDY'S DEPARTURE

BULLHEAD CITY—OCTOBER 2002

Weeks after Pops and Rudy's return from Tijuana, the operatives settled into their respective undercover roles in Bullhead City, spending their days negotiating drug deals, socializing with outlaws, and gasping for downtime, pockets of respite when they could sleep uninterrupted, speak candidly without worrying that one phrase or word might be misinterpreted or taken out of context. In their undercover residence Bird shared floor space with Timmy, Carlos, and Rudy; Pops preferred to curl up by the door. They took turns on night watch, forced to trust each other. But Bird never completely shut down, although he had moments of deep darkness during which he drifted off and the only sound he heard was his own breathing.

In the half-light of dawn, Bird gripped his Sig Sauer, a pall of apprehension filled the air. His pager flashed the time: 3:00 A.M. There it was again, a tapping sound in the corner of the room. Bird scrambled to his feet, suddenly alert. The veins in his arms gnarled like ropes. No movement in the house. He glanced to his side; where the hell was Timmy? Pops mumbled by the window and Bird wasn't sure whether he was awake or asleep. Carlos's shadow stretched along the wall as he stood in the hallway unmoving and trained his eye on Rudy, who sat on the edge of the couch, still dressed in his vest and boots.

The door to the undercover house creaked open in the wind, the dead bolt broken, hanging by a hinge. For a fleeting moment Bird wondered whether Rudy had left the door open on purpose? Rudy was unpredictable, and Bird didn't doubt that Rudy was capable of betrayal. Had he gone out for the evening unbeknownst to the operatives? Surely the surveillance crew would have noticed?

Bird inched, gun drawn, toward the dark shower stall. Water dripped slowly from the faucet and formed a small puddle on the tiles. *Breathe. Just breathe.* A scurry of feet rustled behind him. Bird whipped around, his hands shaking. Out of reflex he nearly fired, caught himself, and watched in dizzy disbelief as a large rat smacked its tail into a sandbag.

A match flared in the darkness as Rudy lit a cigarette. He had made himself comfortable on the couch. "You guys don't know shit about being bikers," he chastised and nodded toward the broken door. He rubbed his nose and cringed as if in pain. Bird suspected Rudy had suffered a post-narcotic ingestion burn.

"That's because we're not bikers you shit head. We're cops," Carlos reminded him. The tension between the two was palpable. He cast Bird a knowing glance. The fucker had pocketed a stash of dope from his last monitored buy and had had the nerve to snort it under their noses. Timmy ran a finger across his throat, signaling what Bird had already acknowledged: Rudy's number was up.

"You think you're something special?" Rudy challenged Carlos. "You ain't better than me. What town you come from in Mexico?" He pressed, nearly inciting Carlos to a brawl, particularly since Carlos was Puerto Rican.

"Knock it off you two." Bird warned, jamming the door shut with a sandbag, as he hatched his plan.

His gaze fell on the scraps of paper lying on the floor, eerily white beneath the bald frosted ceiling bulb: names of Smitty's projected hits, court documents, photographs of a target house and witnesses to question. Smitty knew of Bird's reputation as an assassin/debt collector and had propositioned him earlier in his cramped living room to recover outstanding debts from drug dealers. Lydia had dutifully left the two to discuss business, disappearing through the couple's black-beaded curtain to fetch beer. Smitty leaned forward on his blood-red couch, smiled knowingly at Bird, and whispered conspiratorially, "Do whatever it takes."

Bird nodded, mentally crossing entrapment off his list. He listened to Smitty prattle on, "I spend my time working, drinking, fighting, chasing pussy, and being an asshole," as if Bird could be intimidated. Killing aside, Smitty reminded Bird that he was, first and foremost, a businessman, and as such he expected compensation for his "referrals," a small percentage of the proceeds collected. And he wouldn't balk at a souvenir either, a trophy to add to his achievements on the wall. "I'm thinking of starting a Mohave County chapter of the Hells Angels; I could use a couple of good prospects," Smitty winked, offering Bird the collateral/deposit he thought Bird needed. "You do this for me, and I'll reward you."

The hell you will, Bird thought, his mind racing. Shit, he'd even convinced Smitty he was a hired killer. The real theater was in encouraging Smitty to wait until the heat cooled. Unlike his other murder-for-hire ruses, which he had carefully orchestrated with ATF, Bird couldn't approach Smitty's victims, tell them today was their lucky day, and order the arrest of their hit man. He would spoil the case. Instead, he pacified Smitty, assured him that he *would* collect the debts in good time, when it was safe.

Smitty nodded, adding, "The cops are watching you too."

Bird smothered a smile. The locals *had* begun to question Bird's presence in Bullhead City. They'd gone so far as to draft flyers with Bird's picture on the front. They'd distributed these to task force agents who attended the briefings, and in a bizarre play within a play, task force cops advised the local cops that "they'd look into him."

Good. Bird could use law enforcement's suspicion of him to his advantage. If the cops were watching him, then they could also watch Rudy, particularly if Bird gave them good reason. Not that he had to work too hard; Rudy had already dug his own trench. Trouble was there was only so much Bird could do to shorten Rudy's leash in front of the Hells Angels without attracting their suspicion. He couldn't exactly scold the president of the Solo Angeles nomad chapter for ingesting dope, or getting drunk, or being a general screw-up. After all, Rudy *was* a biker; his *role* was to be a bona fide dick.

"You take orders from me, not the other way around," Bird was firm with Rudy. "I say when you take a piss and when you can go home. Remember that and you might see daylight in this lifetime."

"We have to take him out," Beef advised at a headquarters briefing soon after. The last thing any of them needed was a dirty informant whom they *knew* was dirty. Although Rudy had been instrumental in introducing the operatives to the Hells Angels he was no longer necessary to the operation. But removing him posed its own challenges: The operatives couldn't exactly enlist local cops they didn't trust or know. Rudy's situation was delicate. If the informant blabbed to save his ass, they could all go down.

"We have to do it in a way that looks legitimate," Bird cautioned, knowing that the removal of Rudy would automatically propel him into the status of the Solo club's defacto president, a role that would not only garner the respect of the Hells Angels but also their sympathy.

In the end ATF resorted to re-arresting Rudy on the original gun charge that had first brought the informant to Beef's attention. On a blistering morning in Bullhead City, with the fake Solos traveling four deep on their motorcycles in the coveted first position behind the Hells Angels on their way to a Spartan Motorcycle Club funeral, a police helicopter lit up the sky.

The SWAT team on the ground closed in on Rudy with their weapons drawn, after receiving an anonymous tip that Rudy was loaded. They were dressed in full riot regalia with helmets, vests, shields, and rifles. Bird was sure that none of the SWAT cops had a clue that he was among friends. Their orders were to remove Rudy. Still, Bird and his team were as roughed up as the confidential informant (aka CI). Panic zipped across the informant's face as he flashed Bird a reproachful look, and Bird couldn't help but wonder who had betrayed whom?

Under the watchful eyes of the Hells Angels, Rudy was handcuffed, and busted for weapons and drug violations just weeks after the CI had been stopped by police for possession of drug paraphernalia. It helped that Rudy had quantities of meth concealed in the heel of his shoe.

The media would later twist Rudy's arrest as proof that ATF had lost control of its informant. No one would ever credit the operatives with having executed a well-calculated plan.

FOR THE GOOD OF THE CAUSE

Soon after Rudy's arrest, Beef announced at another midnight briefing at the Pumpkin Patch that the Miami field office demanded Carlos' return. "They can't have him," Bird barked, already wary of his crew's low morale.

"He was only on loan," Beef reminded the group, as if Carlos weren't present.

"Well Jesus Christ," Timmy smacked his hand down on the table, "how's that going to look? We just lost our club president, and now we lose another member? You don't think the Hells Angels are going to get suspicious?"

Beef paced the small quarters, his face flush with irritation. The Solo Angeles were down two full-patched members.

"It's not like we have recruits lining up to replace them," Timmy said, his voice rising an octave. His nerves were already shot. Pops wasn't doing much better; he visibly paled as he stirred a cool cup of black coffee.

"How do you propose we remove him?" Bird asked testily, voicing Beef's concerns. They needed an exit strategy to explain the sudden departure of their only Spanish-speaking member.

"We could devise a ruse where we kill him off," Beef suggested, thinking aloud. "We tell the Hells Angels he's gun running in Mexico and smacks into a telephone pole. We have to leave to go buy him a burial plot. We could pretend we have funeral arrangements to make while we gather reinforcements."

No one was impressed.

Meanwhile, over plates of waffles at the Waffle House the next morning, Pops spilled a story of his own. There was a Mongol living in Kingman, Arizona, who had associates working for him, so-called secret members the Mongol had recruited to solicit Hells Angels prospects to sell methamphetamine supplied by Mongols. Bird used the information to devise an e-mail ruse that contained truthful but generic information related to the activities of Mongol members in Tijuana during the previous week; "It's all about allowing criminals to form an inaccurate conclusion from accurate information."

Bird presented the e-mail to Smitty at the Blemont motorcycle rally the following week, hoping the news would ignite the fire between the Hells Angels and the Mongols. Forming alliances with the Hells Angels against a mutual parasite was integral to Black Biscuit's operation. Bird already had a rapport with Smitty. The biker had foolishly entrusted Bird with debt collections and contract killings. Bird knew that feeding Smitty privileged information about the Hells Angels most hated rival would only elevate Bird's status in the biker club to "confidant," potential prospective Hells Angel "brother," and an all-around contender.

The ruse worked. Smitty, expressing appropriate concern over the increasing Mongol threat, introduced Bird to fellow Hells Angel member and future vice president of the Mohave County Hells Angel chapter, Silent Steve, at Wild Bills, an Angels hangout. Grateful for Bird's tip, Silent Steve offered Bird his teenage daughter as "good company."

"She's good for you to hang out with Bird," Lydia affirmed, squeezing the girl's arm as if she were meat. "She's waited a long time to meet you."

"You've been well received by the brothers," Smitty affirmed.

Bird took a long pull on his beer, nausea churning in his gut as he registered the teenager's feigned seductive pose, her pasty cheeks, and thin, bruised lips. She was Bird's own daughter's age, and he was consumed with pity. Part of him wanted to rescue her; the other part of him wanted to strangle Silent Steve. Instead, he dismissed the girl's advances and jokingly explained, "No offense, but I don't mess with jailbait. She's not even old enough to have a driver's license."

"Hey man, if she's old enough to sit at the table, she's old enough to eat," Silent Steve shrugged.

Bird shook his head and said he had eyes for someone else.

Smitty smiled knowingly, "That blond chick I saw you with in California on the beach?"

Bird's heart raced. By some fluke encounter, he and Special Agent JJ[7], the perky, fresh recruit he'd met at a training confernce in San Diego, had spied Smitty a few weeks earlier with Lydia in San Diego. JJ, fresh out of college and the academy, had slid effortlessly into the role of Bird's "score" for the day. She was perfect, untainted by government bullshit, and she had no sense yet that the Hells Angels were evil incarnate. Instead, JJ viewed the bikers as any former sorority girl might, as fraternity boys with knives. Unfortunately, JJ was just an understudy; the brass was nervous about casting the lead with a rookie. She had never worked undercover, knew nothing about the biker lifestyle, and was too big a risk. But she *looked* the part: well endowed and blond.

"Just what she'd like to hear, hired for her tits," Beef remarked. "She has a good head on her shoulders," Smitty affirmed as if his approval mattered to Bird. "I don't like the one Timmy brought with him. She knows too many people, cops by name. I'll have to get rid of her."

"If they're going to give you a chick, then I get to have one too," Timmy had insisted by Bird. Timmy's little show of defiance had nearly cost them the Belmont rally. Shame it had never crossed Timmy's mind to control his borrowed undercover detective chick and advise her that wearing a black boa around her neck might not be the wisest choice when riding on the back of a motorcycle.

"I'm sure she gets it now," Carlos had roared after the woman's boa snarled Timmy's exhaust pipes and caused Timmy to dump his bike in a cluster of barrel cactus. Lucky for him, the ATF trailer that had hauled their bikes within a few miles of the rally wasn't too far away; after some

---

[7] Undercover name.

choice language, Beef gave Timmy a substitute bike and hauled the trashed one away for repairs.

Smitty soon tired of the subject of women, and, eager to impress his new confidant, bragged about his credentials and why it was only appropriate that *he* should head the new nomad chapter of the Hells Angels in Mohave County. After all, Smitty had paid his dues to the club at the Laughlin Harrah's Casino, where he had served as a Hells Angel scout, hunting for Mongols, ready and willing, without provocation, to "blow their fucking heads off." Smitty added matter-of-factly to Bird, "That's what brothers do for each other, act as human shields. That's what the cause is all about."

Bird nodded. He understood what Smitty meant by "the cause." Bird never lost sight of *his* role either—the Hells Angles were not his allies. "They'll kill you in a heartbeat," Bird reminded his team and snapped his fingers. "Just like that."

Bird seized the opportunity to further the cause a few days later at the Hells Angels "Five Year Anniversary Party" held at the Mesa clubhouse. "Good, you can take Marla[8] with you," Beef said, introducing Bird to his first government issued "girlfriend," ATF special agent Marla Holmes. Bird had complained once too often that if ATF didn't provide him with a female foil soon, the government would have a lot of explaining to do when Bird eventually testified that he resisted temptation time and time again without repercussion. "The allegations are going to be made that I laid a ton of women to keep my cover," Bird insisted to Beef after he received ATF's initial predictable rejections—a female plant was expensive, unnecessary, and a luxury.

"How big a price does ATF want to pay for stupidity?" Bird warned. Like it or not, women were the ultimate test in the biker world. Bird could maneuver the drug issue, make excuses that he didn't mix business with pleasure, that he needed a clear head to do arms deals, but women . . . they were a different story. No hot-blooded American male could resist sex and get away with it . . . unless he already had a woman of his own—an actual physical presence, not just a phantom "old lady" in Tucson with two kids

---

[8] Pseudonym.

he rarely saw. If nothing else at least it would ease Barbara's concerns. Not that she ever mentioned it directly, but Bird didn't need more issues between them, more fog and awkward silences as they learned to connect again for brief moments of respite. He was the phantom husband/father, appearing at will in his family's life and disappearing almost as quickly, after pretending—for a while—to slip into a normal routine: mowing the lawn, helping with his son with their homework. At times it felt as if *that* were his undercover life, his assumed identity.

Perhaps Bird should have been more specific when he pled his case to the ATF: he would have preferred a woman who wouldn't get him killed. Bird examined Marla Holmes with a critical eye and inwardly cringed. She wasn't exactly "biker chick" material. She was too . . . seasoned and smelled of cop. Stiff. Tall and lanky. Marla shook Bird's hand with conviction. Her short hair barely moved. Marla had never worked undercover in her entire career, and Bird wasn't about to train her. He shot Beef a reproachful glance and said to Marla, "Let's take it slowly, see how it goes."

An Angels anniversary bash probably wasn't the best venue to introduce Marla to the club but . . . The Mesa clubhouse was crawling with Hells Angels, among them, Ghost, Big Head, Lonesome Lonnie, Joby, Chef Boy Are Dee, Egg Head, and Mac, the "artiste" who tattooed Bird in his dive parlor located a block south of the federal building. Mac wore a wig because he had a nonassociation[9] clause on his probation sentence prohibiting contact with felons.

Some of the Hells Angels members who attended the mixer couldn't afford a baloney sandwich. They grabbed meal scraps and a hot shower at Bird's undercover residence. Others had flown in from Europe for the special occasion. All were armed—thanks to Ghost's relaxed rules—with double shoulder holsters and a loaded Benelli shotgun.

Bird flashed Mesa Bob's special invitation to Ghost, and he escorted the operatives to the segregated picnic tables on the back patio. Crow, another member, motioned for them to take a seat. Timmy and Marla ex-

---

[9] A nonassociation clause means that as a felon, Mac was prohibited by his probation officer from socializing with other felons or he would be in violation of his probation. He was also not permitted to identify himself as a Hells Angel.

cused themselves and detoured toward the restrooms inside where Lydia cornered Marla. Unfortunately, Lydia had made Bird her special match-making project and quickly whisked Marla away for questioning. Dope would inevitably be a part of any girl talk, and Bird instinctively cringed. The whole operation suddenly hinged on a woman. Timmy, suspecting trouble, took his cue from Bird's anxious stare and lingered outside the stall hoping to run interference when the two females finally emerged.

Bird spied Ghost inside the clubhouse surrounded by a host of female groupies, his leg in a cast, white rocks, the size of small baseballs, spread across the table, powder sprinkled around them. Bird watched as one female lowered her face into the mixture, inhaled deeply, and ingested a large portion of the narcotics. Mesa Bob caught Bird's eye, grinned, and made the sound of a train whistle, signaling the start of group sex.

Hells Angel George Walters, aka "Joby," drew his pistol from his waist-band, pointed the gun at the head of a pesky female looking to score dope, and yelled, "I'll kill you bitch." The woman scurried off like a rat into the dark corners of the clubhouse. Bird caught Pops's anxious old eyes across the table. They had an agenda to cover; the night was young, but the atmosphere was turning ugly fast. None of them needed to witness another night of boozing and sex. Bird's nerves were already shot. They'd all gone at least twenty-four hours with no sleep. He nursed his beer as Timmy and Marla waded back through the crowd to his table.

One of the wives rolled a joint and offered it to Marla as she slid next to Bird. Marla visibly tensed. Bird took that as his cue and signaled for Bob to join them. Maybe no one would notice that his old lady didn't quite blend. After all, women were just props to these guys. The wife scowled, shrugged, and made a concerted effort to blow smoke into Marla's face for the rest of the evening. Bird feared the woman might drop a pill into Marla's beer just for fun.

Bob grabbed one last squeeze of a woman's ass before joining Bird at the picnic table. Bird produced a sealed envelope and slid it to Mesa Bob.

"A gift for you, from the Solos."

Mesa Bob opened the envelope, examined the bills inside, pocketed the mock business card that read, "Love and Respect, Solos," and wrote on the envelope, "Solos donation." He nodded, visibly pleased. He leaned forward and said in a low whisper, "You guys have to bring Rudy back in."

Bird took the bait. He had the perfect opportunity to cast Bob in the role of mentor. "My men are feeling pretty down. They need a pep talk. Without a president they feel lost. What would you do if you were in my situation?"

Flattery worked. Bob beamed at the invitation to puff up Bird. In an unexpected show of affection, he stood, knocked over his metal chair, and gathered Pops, Timmy, and Carlos into a huddle.

"Follow Bird's lead and do what he says."

Extricating Carlos from the mix proved easier than expected. A week after the anniversary bash, an article hit the *Arizona Republic* involving a renowned dope smuggler named Pedro Jimenez.

"It's perfect," Beef said, spreading the article on the table at Black Biscuit's headquarters. "You'll start a rumor with the Hells Angels that Carlos is Pedro's uncle, that Carlos is worried the cops will come sniffing around *him* and bring heat to the Solos and necessarily to the Hells Angels, and that Carlos is willing to lay down his life's dream to become a patched Hells Angel for the good of the cause and disappear for a while. Maybe he'll head to San Juan."

It was always a good idea to keep as close to the truth as possible when crafting an undercover story. After all, Carlos *was* being relocated to Puerto Rico on assignment. The whole telephone pole smashup and search for a burial plot ruse simply didn't ring true. But Carlos fleeing to Puerto Rico to save the Hells Angels from unwanted scrutiny could work, especially on the heels of Rudy's arrest. After all, as Mesa Bob was fond of reminding Bird, Carlos's "sacrifice" was just "brothers helping brothers" for the "good of the cause." It helped that Carlos sent postcards with a San Juan postmark.

BAIT

In the week that followed Carlos's departure, Bird was restless. He faced another dawn without sleep. His undercover house in Bullhead City was too quiet. Pops had slumped over on the floor, his lips blue with worry and cold. Bird didn't dare startle him awake—Pops had begun to hallucinate and see spirits in the halls. The old CI insisted that his visions were real and began to spew spirit messages, warnings from the grave that the end was near. Bird sensed something too—not supernatural, and perhaps that was what frightened him the most. Bird knew that Beef had intelligence from Hells Angels in California who distrusted the sudden formation of the nomad Solo Angeles in Arizona, and worried that Bird was becoming too close to high-ranking Hells Angels officials. Beef warned Bird that trouble was brewing.

Bird scanned the empty streets outside his window like a hunter searching for potential prey. Soon it would be Thanksgiving. His breath frosted the glass. A purplish plume spread over the horizon like a bruise. Timmy scrunched on the couch, his hands twitching from restless sleep. True to his outlaw role, he still wore his boots. Always be prepared for trouble. It was a wise precaution. They could never let their guard down. At any given moment they could have a night visitor. Only the surveillance cameras posted on the roof gave them warning.

Bird guessed that only Marla Holmes was resting peacefully in her own bed, her brief stint as an undercover biker chick having ended by mutual agreement. No hard feelings. He couldn't blame her. Still, part of him was reluctant to lose her. He might wait weeks for an understudy. It wasn't as if ATF had viable players eager to audition for the role. Bird petitioned for JJ. She already had a nod from Smitty and Lydia. She just might work.

Bird chewed a cuticle, his nerves shot. The first signs of life stirred in the streets. A young boy, close to his son's age, wandered outside, kicked a smashed beer can with his bare foot, and lifted the lid to his neighbor's dumpster. Bird watched him, morbidly fascinated, rooted to his post by insomnia, suddenly unsure what was real and what was dreamscape. Hot wind blew the boy's hair from his eyes as he turned, chewed drumstick in hand, looking one hundred years old.

Shaken, Bird moved away from the window and headed for the restroom. A shower might do him good. But then he remembered the last person who had used the stall—"Harley Angel"—the toddler of a visiting Hells Angel. The baby's body had been blood-raw from scavies. Bird recalled how the child's father had held the toddler's hand in the shower as he guided cold water over the baby's face and stomach.

Bird balanced his gun on the sink and splashed ice water on his face. His reflection in the chipped glass startled him—months of living like an animal had made him look like one: unkempt goatee, bald head, glazed blue eyes like a wolf's, and a second skin of ink. No wonder his wife recoiled from his appearance; it wasn't as if he could ever clean up on his rare visits home. At least his children were forgiving. Bird would always be "Dad" to them, no matter how monstrous he looked.

Bird steadied his hands on the sink as another wave of dizziness passed. His diet of stress, beer, and coffee was taking its toll. And now he wasn't even sure the operation could thrive with just three Pumpkins. He stumbled out of the bathroom. Timmy stirred awake. Pops laced up his boots and gave Bird a sober nod. He was off to Tijuana again to pay their membership dues. Alone. Bird didn't want to think about the fate of Operation Black Biscuit if Pops didn't return.

★ ★ ★

Beef shoved the coffee pot in Bird's face at headquarters the next morning. No one complained that the brew was cold and stale. Attendance at the Pumpkin Patch had dwindled to ten. The surveillance team was now bigger than the operatives. Morale was low. Not even Buddha, one of the surveillance crew, smiled. But there was one new face at the table, special agent "JJ" sat next to Beef and grinned broadly at the motley crew. She wasn't exactly the reinforcement people expected. The twenty-nine-year-old recruit oozed enthusiasm, and unlike Marla, who was a liability, JJ was just naive enough about the Hells Angels to deflect attention.

Bird registered Timmy's disappointment, and Beef's quiet resignation at JJ's presence. *It is what it is,* Bird accepted. He knew it would take time to recruit new Solo members; those who fit the bill were either slightly crazy or too stupid to know better. Working deep cover took a special dedication.

Bird could almost hear his wife's retort echo in his head, "Is that what you call it?" Maybe Barbara was right. It wasn't dedication. It was pure selfishness for the "good of the cause." He was no different than his biker enemies; single-minded determination kept them both alive. The comparisons chilled him. Maybe it was semantics, but JJ seemed to have both, dedication and selfishness, and something even more valuable: she was single with no children. JJ wouldn't have to worry about telling half-truths to her loved ones, believing that the less they knew the better, that knowing too much could only hurt them.

One week later, after a day of pacifying anxious debt collectors and working out last-minute details in his murder-for-hire cases, Bird arranged to meet with Smitty at the Inferno Lounge, a notorious biker haven in Bullhead City. Rows of Harleys crowded the parking lot like metal guards.

Unease settled over Bird as he idled his engine searching for an empty space to park his hog. JJ gripped his waist, her fingers twisting through the loose threads of his vest as she straddled the bike. In the near darkness Timmy's face contorted, sweat moistening his cheeks. The only lights glowed from twin torch lamps at the entrance. Bird met the menacing stares of tattooed, leather-clad Hells Angels whose thrill it was to kill and took a deep breath.

Bird parked his bike, dismounted, and hoped his knees wouldn't buckle from tension. He caught JJ's eyes. Panic surged through him. The Solos were already dwindling in numbers. He didn't need another downer. If JJ didn't work . . . if she blew his cover . . . if she didn't blend the way he expected, it was over. She winked at him and Bird shivered despite the oppressive heat. If she could just keep her story straight, they might be okay. She was supposed to be his "driver," a role most women played in the biker world that not only gave them purpose but also allowed them to accessorize and wear a gun.

Apart from being mere eye candy and a biker's property, women served another useful purpose: at a moment's notice they obediently stashed the bikers' weapons and dope in a van they drove behind the motorcycles in case the cops pulled them over. In this way the women demonstrated their loyalty to the club; *they* would take the fall for the bikers—most of whom were prohibited possessors—even risk prison for dope possession.

Inside, the bar felt like an inferno. Thundering heavy metal pumped through the place. Shadows masked the faces of several heavily tattooed bikers, most of whom were Hells Angels and fringe club supporters like the Vagos, who recoiled at the Solos as if they had a foul smell. Bird knew better than to avoid their cold stares. Intimidation was a tactic bikers used to weed out the weak . . . or to identify cops. Show no fear.

Timmy panted behind him, a physical manifestation of the stress they all masked. Family tensions distracted Timmy, made him irritable. He bristled at Bird's instructions and resented his leadership—they were supposed to be a team, an ensemble cast.

Pops looked close to death in the milky darkness. Bird felt his presence like a phantom limb. Tension bulged like ropes in Pops's neck. His trips to Tijuana were numbered; like a participant in a Mexican roulette, he sensed it was just a matter of time before his cover unraveled. A white boy in the midst of a hundred Hispanic bikers was more than a little suspicious. And now Pops traveled alone, without Rudy's buffer or impossible chatter. A muscle in Pops's jaw ticked and his hands shook like a man with Parkinson's. Time was running out for all of them. If Bird didn't strike fast, he would lose his chance.

A spiral staircase wound upstairs and divided the bar into two kinds of clientele: drinkers and "businessmen." Women fell into the first category. They were party favors, property, sex toys. They often lingered behind, mingled with the other wives or girlfriends, ingested dope in the bathrooms, or simply waited to be useful. Here, they leaned against the walls like exotic vines and watched with detached interest as various bikers bid on them as part of their pool game.

Smitty appeared from a dark hole at the end of the bar and signaled to the bouncers at the door that Bird and his team were his guests. Without further protest, Smitty ushered the Pumpkins upstairs, including JJ. The group slid onto red vinyl stools.

Smitty ordered a round of beer and informed Bird that he had a hot tip: two Mongols were living in Bullhead City and he needed the Solos help to "take them out." Never mind that the Solos had just lost their president. This was a test—would Bird accept his challenge? Would he kill for the club and for the "good of the cause"? More importantly, would Bird take the fall for Smitty if things backfired? Smitty had made it clear—he would not return to prison.

Before Bird could muster an answer, JJ wedged between them.

Whether it was her blissful ignorance of Hells Angels protocol or her complete disregard for her designated role as Bird's property, she piqued Smitty's curiosity in a way that none of the other female plants had. Her breezy manner, infectious laugh, and confident sexuality oozed appeal. But as attractive as JJ was, Smitty's hands didn't roam. She was Bird's girl. Enough said.

"I'm not often impressed with women," Bird overheard Smitty's conversation with JJ, "but I like the way you handle yourself."

"I'd be willing to help you," JJ said and quickly clarified. "As a driver I could stash your stuff for you." She was good. Blend. Mix. In less than two hours, she'd earned what it had taken Bird months to acquire: Smitty's respect.

Bird sipped his beer quietly, the corner of his mouth lifting slightly as Smitty leaned closer to JJ and whispered confidentially, "Stick with Bird. He'll likely be a Hells Angel in the near future."

WIRED

Bird decided to repeat his success in Bullhead City with Mesa Hells Angels president Mesa Bob and arranged an impromptu meeting with him at a 5 and Diner restaurant in Chandler partly to clarify Bird's position to the Hells Angels as the Solos' new de-facto club president, but more importantly, to seek Johnston's help in securing the blessing of a bigger Hells Angel player, Daniel "Hoover" Seybert, the president of Sonny Barger's Cave Creek Hells Angel chapter, who had originally been less than accepting of the Solos presence in Arizona. Mesa Bob pledged to Bird that he would do anything to help Bird, including spreading the news to Hoover that the Solos had permission to exist in Arizona as Johnston's guests. Bird's generous cash donation to the Mesa Hells Angels' defense fund solidified Johnston's promise although Bird insisted it was "just brothers helping brothers."

Bird knew Mesa Bob was no fool. The club boss didn't care about the fate of the Solo Angeles in Arizona following the loss of their club president—Mesa Bob cared about business. He cared about Bird's ability to thrive and continue to traffic arms for the Hells Angels into Mexico. Mesa Bob needed Bird's connections. The *Hells Angels* needed Bird. All it took was one phone call to Hoover from Mesa Bob and Hoover, too, welcomed Bird into his criminal fraternity.

★ ★ ★

But the Hells Angels would soon have to cool their gun-running exploits. Club spies buzzed that a Las Vegas grand jury was preparing to indict members of the Hells Angels for the April Harrah's Casino shootout with the Mongols. Prosecutors had seized an "enhanced" version of the shootout video and thousands of pages of supporting documents.

An agitated Mesa Bob deferred all arms trafficking negotiations to the Red Devils. The support club had previously negotiated drug buys with Rudy. What difference would it make to simply offer the outlaws a substitute? Timmy. It wasn't as if the Red Devils had a rapport with Rudy. At least secretly that's what Timmy hoped. Primed for the role of a lifetime, Timmy would get the chance to fly solo to be deep cover *alone*. Sure he had spent years working narcotics cases with the Phoenix Police Department, but those had been small time, hand-to-hand sales and drug deals in the zoo parking lot or in a strip mall in broad daylight. But this, this was what he had wanted from the beginning, to be part of the "guts" and the pulse that moved undercover cops to a primitive beat.

While Timmy's zeal was admirable, it was also foolish. Bird lectured him like an older brother, worried that Timmy was too green, too caught up in a Hollywood ideal of what it meant to be undercover. "Don't go in there like you're fucking Serpico," Bird admonished Timmy at a headquarters meeting. "We should wait for Pops to return from Mexico," Bird suggested, fearful that Timmy's enthusiasm would have disastrous consequences.

"Timmy will be fine," Beef said, by way of dismissing Bird's protests.

"He hasn't slept in days," Bird added.

Beef arched a brow at Bird as if that detail hardly mattered. None of them had slept well since the investigation started. Timmy paced nightly like a wild animal in a cell, afraid to curl up or drop his guard. With only two other Solo Angeles to choose from, Pops stuck in Tijuana and Bird too visible, Timmy was the plant. Paranoia laced Timmy's cockiness as he argued with Beef over having to wear a wire.

The Red Devils president, Tony, arranged to meet Timmy at a bar, Peppers, at noon. Unease itched up the back of Bird's neck as he watched Timmy from his safe vantage point inside the surveillance van pull his hog into the bar's empty parking lot. Bird had argued with Beef, insisting that he be allowed to monitor the deal since it was Timmy's first transaction alone.

Tony was seated in a gold Honda Accord smoking a cigarette. Not what Bird expected from an outlaw *biker*. Tony, dressed casually in a black T-shirt, jeans, and dark sunglasses with painted flames on the sides, stepped out of the car, slammed the door shut, and flicked his cigarette butt to the ground. His boots crunched on the gravel as he marched up to Timmy and ordered him to dismount. His arms were like loaves of bread, studded at the wrists with Red Devils leather bands imprinted with the club's insignia. Prison tattoos webbed his neck. Bird knew Timmy was in trouble after Tony informed him that the bar didn't open until 1:00 P.M. "Let's go for a ride."

It wasn't a suggestion.

In the van Bird shot Beef a hard look. If things didn't change soon, they'd be forced to rescue Timmy. In a flash the investigation would be over, all of their efforts suddenly reduced to nothing.

"What did you need to meet about?" Tony barked, peeling away from the bar.

Timmy's voice was small and tight as he explained that Rudy had been arrested and was currently facing federal weapons charges that stemmed from a two-year-old case. "He told me to get in touch with you to buy guns and wheels."[10]

Tony nodded. As he drove, his eyes darted to his left and right mirrors. He steered the car down numerous alleys, dodging main streets in what simulated countersurveillance techniques. Eventually, he stopped on a side street. A large Hispanic male, a full-patched member of the Red Devils whom Tony introduced to Timmy as "James," appeared from the shadows. He approached the car and ordered Timmy to exit. Once outside, James pushed Timmy toward a cluster of garbage cans. The alley was deserted. Timmy caught the cold black stare of a pigeon, his only witness. Tony frisked him, patting Timmy's waist, clawing at his shirt, running his hands down Timmy's legs. "Wait," Timmy protested. Bird swallowed and strained his eyes to see past the van's dirty windows as Timmy pulled his

---

[10] Slang for stolen cars and motorcycles.

pants to his ankles. James smirked, nodded his approval, apparently satisfied that Timmy was not wired.

"We have to be sure man. It's cool."

Timmy's close call with Tony prompted Beef to take a bold risk and eliminate the use of wires in certain situations. Given the constant scrutiny and the unpredictable nature of the outlaws, the decision to wear a wire would, in most circumstances, prove to be suicidal. But it was a judgment call that each operative had to make based on any given situation, and it was a balancing act—safety versus evidence preservation. Timmy had nearly compromised the entire investigation. Had the Red Devils discovered his wire, he would have been executed.

As a precaution, after his close call, Beef ordered Timmy to take a few hours off, visit the wife, step into a normal routine to get some relief. But Timmy refused, opting instead to mope around headquarters and play with Beef's caged lizard. Bird couldn't blame him. He sensed that Timmy hadn't yet mastered the skill of slipping in and out of two worlds unnoticed and unscathed. Sometimes it was easier to live in darkness rather than to have to explain his existence to his wife and field unnecessary questions. Even Bird, as experienced as he was, had difficulty moving between worlds. The lines were blurry. Bird recalled his own close encounter just weeks earlier when, on an impromptu visit home, he'd taken his daughter to Home Depot and bumped into a Hells Angel.

"This is my kid. I'm visiting my old lady," Bird bluffed.

That was the trick, staying as close to the truth as possible without blowing his cover. Thankfully, his daughter didn't flinch. Instead she nodded, as interested as any teenager could be at meeting her parent's friends. She didn't need to know she was part of Bird's story.

Beef's risky decision to forego wires in certain situations paid off. Bird narrowly escaped a similar fate days later when Tony asked *him* to drop his pants in the Peppers Cantina urinal. Never mind that he was the *third* Solo Angeles in as many days to prove to the club that he wasn't a cop. Or that he was accompanied by Tucson Hells Angel chapter member, Douglas Dam, aka "Dee," who hours before had proudly displayed and sold to

Bird a series of shotguns and SKS assault weapons he'd concealed between bed sheets in the back of his truck.

With the stench of urine lingering in the air in the Peppers Cantina bathroom, Tony pitched his plan to organize a large-scale drug and firearms smuggling effort south of the border. Timmy was to serve as the Red Devils contact and make arrangements for the purchase and transfer of merchandize. Bird was to ensure their safe transport in a Solo Angeles van.

Cool wind skimmed Bird's bald head as he mounted his motorcycle in the bar's parking lot. Tony watched him leave, staring him down with the black oily gaze of a spider. Did Tony know Bird's secret? Did Tony suspect Bird was a team of two? Had the Red Devil puffed him up to get his guard down?

Bird cranked his bike, cast a final glance at Tony in his rearview mirror, acknowledged Dee's satisfied grin in the bar's doorway, and sped into the gravel road. Had dropping his pants in the urinal been a test, confirmation to Dee that Bird wasn't a cop? As much as he wanted to head home to Barbara, he didn't dare. Instead, he listened for the sound of betrayal: a bullet ripping through the darkness, an engine revving behind him, cackles of laughter. Paranoia gripped him as he steered his bike into desert brush, his boots studded with cactus needles. After nineteen years working undercover, Bird had learned to trust no one. Adrenaline pumped through him like a drug, and although he knew intellectually that he had backup and protection, ultimately, Bird understood that he *really* had no one.

HOLIDAY CHEER

Thanksgiving Day weekend in Bullhead City, the Pumpkins had been invited to attend the wedding of Chef Boy Are Dee and Dolly. Guests were expected to dress in full biker regalia for the occasion and ride in unison to the Riviera Baptist Church. The idea that a Hells Angel would even want to make anything legal was perverse particularly since their creed was to "fuck the world." Still, Bird played along, pleased that Chef thought enough of his brood to include them on the guest list.

At least they were making progress.

Cold rain spit against Bird's face as he gathered his team of Pumpkins outside the Inferno Lounge to wait for the Hells Angels to arrive. Chef's wedding was scheduled to begin in thirty minutes though Bird didn't expect punctuality. Pops's lips had turned a pale blue. His last trip to Tijuana hadn't gone so well. The Solos were asking too many questions and their international president, Suzuki, still wanted his motorcycle. Timmy's expression was stoic. Tension bit through the chill as soaked and shivering Bird absorbed his team's silent reprimands. Not only were they still without reinforcements, but they were also spending the holidays with the Hells Angels. It was one thing to be undercover alone—if plans failed or the investigation soured the blame was Bird's—but saddling him with the responsibility of a whole team was another burden altogether and the pressure was debilitating. A muscle in Bird's jaw ticked. Sooner or later the Hells Angels would pry . . . no matter how much they liked Bird.

Smitty and Silent Steve emerged from the bar soaked in beer. They'd started the celebrations early. They nodded toward the Solos and staggered to their bikes. Chef and Dolly followed, supporting each other as they gave a loud excited "whoop."

Bird and his team traveled in unison on slick wet roads inhaling motorcycle exhaust and oil, with rain streaming down their faces. The sound of engines was deafening. JJ shifted behind him, strands of her long wet hair whipping at his cheeks. She was the team's wild card. JJ had the kind of all-American open face that absorbed secrets. Her charm was arresting. "Good women are hard to find," Lydia reminded Bird. "The club knows that women can cause problems. JJ keeps her mouth shut."

Bird quickly learned that women were integral to the recruiting process. While some were disposable commodities, others served as club scouts. Marriage was a woman's pledge of loyalty to the club's lifestyle, her promise to obey, honor, and accept prison if necessary for the good of the cause. As Bird dripped in the church pew, he watched the ritual unfold with morbid fascination and secretly wondered how many in the room had shared Chef's wife and what dark secrets Dolly sealed at the altar.

Bird threw a wedding reception for the newlyweds at his undercover house, hoping to gather intelligence. The women had settled into a cluster of sandbags to gossip; the men shook bottles of beer and sprayed one another. The scene was an old film spliced together with clips from a nightmare. Bird had prepared a mock e-mail detailing generic biker intelligence related to the Mongols that dovetailed nicely with Lydia's abrupt announcement that crowds of Mongols had been spotted in Laughlin, Nevada. A scout had left her the news on a telephone voice message, and like a good soldier reporting to her general, she spread the warning. With her hands on her hips, she displayed her pistol, assumed a protective stance around the women, and advised Bird that "her main objective was to protect JJ."

"We need to be prepared for war," Smitty cautioned, tipping his beer into the kitchen sink. "Stay straight in case the shooting gets started." He snapped his fingers at Lydia who took his cue and tossed a .38 revolver to

Hells Angel scout Eric, the club's source for hallucinogenic mushrooms. Another good soldier, Eric immediately left the party and borrowed Smitty's Buick to hunt Mongols. Smitty meanwhile reviewed Bird's e-mail, frowned, cocked his head to the side, and ordered Bird to follow him into a back bedroom where they could discuss business.

Smitty, appearing more anxious than usual, whipped out his laser-sighted Taurus pistol and targeted the red beam against the wall. He was prepared for battle armed with two shotguns and an Intratec Tec-9, but he wanted more . . . he wanted Bird to introduce him to his firearms silencer manufacturer. And he wanted Bird's promise that the Solos would fight the Mongols for their brothers.

"The Mohave Valley charter is close to being approved," Smitty volunteered, moving the beam into a bull's-eye. "I'd like you to be my Prospect."

As tempting as the offer was, Bird deferred his answer. Instead he purchased the Taurus from Smitty for $450 and stalled for time. "If they show up here, we're going to kill them," Smitty said, clicking his teeth matter-of-factly, staring at Bird in the blue-dark of the bedroom.

Just after midnight Bird bribed his dead-tired team with waffles at the Denny's Restaurant off Highway 95 in Bullhead City. Bird needed a plan they could all follow before they wound up at the center of a nasty gun fight. In the biker world participating in criminal exploits was part of the patch work, a badge of membership. While drug use and sales was rampant, killing another outlaw required premeditation.

Smitty was not about to return to prison.

Bird understood that if he wanted to *be* a Hells Angel, he would be expected to kill for the club. He knew it was just a matter of time before he encountered a Mongol and was expected to execute him. If he hesitated even a fraction, the operation was over, all their efforts worthless.

Pops's hands shook as he lifted his coffee mug, whether from drugs or alcohol Bird couldn't be sure, but he wasn't interested in knowing the details. Timmy looked worn, his skin pasty and cracked. But his eyes were alert, listening, searching. JJ, who had spent most of the evening chatting with Dolly about marriage and the price of methamphetamine, remarkably exhibited no signs of strain.

The women had their own strange hierarchy, though all were treated like animals. Dolly was among the highest ranking mamas (aka "Sheep" and "Old Ladies") because she had endured the longest and not necessarily with *one* member. Typically, the established women like Dolly, who had paid their dues servicing any member who asked, despised the "thrill seekers"—drug addicts, runaways, so-called biker groupies—who showed up uninvited to motorcycle runs and club parties. These new arrivals were often subjected to sex "tests" of endurance and loyalty, impromptu "humping sessions" that sometimes evolved into orgies.

The women who survived the degradation eventually became the property and "old lady" of one particular member. The "good-lookers" were reserved for high-ranking members, while the less-alluring women were given to prospects or lower-ranking Hells Angels with the understanding that they were club property to be shared. But even the "good mamas" who endured the abuse were expendable; the Hells Angels used the women as drivers or mules to conceal and smuggle weapons and drugs across the border. The women also provided the members with a permanent address so that they could collect welfare if necessary.

Dolly, who was considered a "good mama," was still subjected to club punishment, to beating, gang bangs, or worse if she misbehaved, interrupted her old man's conversation, openly criticized another Hells Angel, or even expressed her own opinion about a particular issue. Still, being a bride had *some* benefits—Dolly was now *Chef's* property and no longer required to service other members (unless Chef ordered it). And she was allowed to carry a fully loaded gun.

Dolly considered JJ an equal, another "good mama" who had paid her dues and earned her status as Bird's old lady. She offered JJ a way to handle the many prison pen pals in Bird's life—the postcards and letters Bird received from fictitious women convicts and narco-terrorists he purposely tossed in plain view in their undercover house to create the illusion that Bird was worshipped.

Dolly ushered JJ into the bathroom, unpinned a small bag of meth from inside her shirt, and offered to sell it to her for $60 dollars. But JJ deferred to Bird; he was in charge of the cash. Dolly offered JJ a lipstick and giggled, "I hide the shit inside my makeup and in ink pens. You should try it." Bird wouldn't approve of dope ingestion, JJ advised, thankful that she had an excuse.

Before the operatives could compare more intelligence, Eric arrived unannounced at the Denny's and slid into the booth across from Bird. His eyes were hooded like a fish's and cloudy with cataracts. His speech was manic, and his gestures so dramatic that he nearly toppled Pops's coffee. He needed fellow hunters to help him scout out the Laughlin casinos in search of Mongols. Eric tapped Bird's shoulder, careful not to touch his patch and stated, "*You're* an assassin." True. But flattery wasn't going to work. Bird volunteered Pops and Timmy . . . for the good of the cause.

Unfortunately, that wasn't Eric's only request.

He also needed a place to stay.

At three o'clock in the morning, Bird startled awake to find Pops towering over him in the darkness shaking uncontrollably. "What the fuck?" Bird protested, his heart racing as he stole a nervous glance at Eric who was happily snoring on a sandbag. Pops's eyes rolled back in his head and for a moment Bird feared that the old CI was having a drug seizure, or more likely, a flashback hallucination from his previous LSD and mushroom use. Bird scrambled to his feet and shook Pops.

"Get a hold of yourself," Bird's voice was a tight whisper.

"Did you see him?" Pops choked. Panic laced through Bird as he pushed Pops aside, gripped his Sig Sauer from inside his boot, and inched toward the front door. He couldn't risk paging Beef. Not with Eric just feet away. Timmy, who never slept, took Bird's silent cue and crawled across the sawdust toward the hallway. JJ for the first time looked rattled, confused, and painfully aware that Eric just might have been a Hells Angel plant.

"Do you see anything?" Timmy's voice cut through the darkness.

Pops moaned and stuffed his face into a sandbag.

Where was the surveillance crew? Why hadn't they tried to call? Had they sensed trouble inside? *Beef, you fucker, you're supposed to be watching out for us.* Adrenaline shot through Bird. Seconds became minutes. He strained his eyes against the darkness to see a shape, a figure in the street.

Nothing. Bird shook his head slowly at Timmy. Had Pops been mistaken? Movement inside. Bird snapped his head toward the sandbags and met Eric's cold penetrating stare.

"Did you see him?" Terror laced Pops's voice.

"See who?" Eric frowned.

"The Devil."

CHRISTMAS RUSH

In the weeks before Christmas, Bird spent his days purchasing an arsenal of weapons from the Hells Angels, "exotics" (fully automatic rifles), SKS assault rifles with bayonets and flash suppressors, hunting rifles with bi-pods on the barrel and homemade silencers consisting of metal tubes stuffed with steel wool, machine guns, Taurus pistols, and dirty Sig Sauers that were once used in criminal exploits. Dee advised Bird that a source in Tucson was manufacturing "bull pup"-type machine guns at the rate of one per week. Possession alone would result in at least a twenty-year prison term. But Dee assured Bird that he would be well rewarded for any risks he took—Craig Kelly, aka "Fang," had invited Bird to prospect for the Tucson Hells Angels charter.

Although it was the goal of Black Biscuit to infiltrate the Hells Angels, Bird had to be careful which fraternity he chose. Since Hells Angel prospects generally served as club property for one year, Bird needed a charter with few members and more relaxed rules, one that would allow Bird to rise through the ranks quickly and become full-patched.

At least as a Solo Angeles, Bird could still call the shots, arrange arms deals with the Hells Angels, offer up his undercover house if necessary, and build walls of trust between the clubs. Bird's strategy worked. In the wee hours of the morning, Bird, who was riding in tandem with JJ behind Dee and Dee's prospect on his motorcycle, was pulled over at gunpoint for fail-ing to obey a stop sign.

Although the stop was just a legal excuse for the locals to inspect the Hells Angels up close, handcuff them, toss them into the spit cage of their patrol car, and detain them for further questioning, Bird worried that the locals might blow his cover. The cops were not privy to ATF's operation or to Bird's undercover role. Strategically, Bird elected not to inform the locals. It was more credible if the cops harassed Bird and his team. Besides, Bird couldn't trust the locals to keep his identity a secret. He had heard ru-mors that the Hells Angels had "friends" inside the department, moles who reported regularly to club members about intelligence the cops might have on them.

"They've developed an unnatural interest in your background," Dee divulged to Bird. "They've been asking questions."

Bird and the operatives sat dutifully silent as the locals scrutinized their fake credentials and backgrounds, scribbled the inane details of their crim-inal exploits on a notepad, and huddled in a cube of bright light to confer. As tempting as it was to calm the shattered nerves of the cops with the news that they had hooked their own, Bird bit his lower lip and assumed the role of an arms trafficker. His federal persona lay hidden far away in a vault at headquarters. Bird communicated silent warnings to JJ—*Say nothing.* JJ ac-knowledged him with a flick of her eyes. She knew better than to impro-vise. Pops and Timmy fixated on a ripple of dirt as they stood with their hands splayed across their government-issued Mercury Cougar.

The only sound in the patrol car was the prospect's uneven breathing as the cops demanded he produce registration for his motorcycle. Bird's mind raced with questions they had yet to answer—Where were they headed? Where had they come from? What did they have in the back of their trunk? And how would he ensure that their stories meshed? It was one thing to be stopped alone and interrogated, but detained with a whole team . . . that just invited trouble. There was no way their stories would be the same.

Pops was already unstable, misguided by his ghostly visions, and Timmy was a live wire waiting to sizzle. Bird shivered. The cold morning air chilled him. He had no clear focus, only dim fog, and he was so damn tired. Part of him wished for the relief of a jail cell where he could curl up for a couple of hours and sleep.

No expectations.

No pressure.

Just pure caged bliss.

But Dee's prospect was the "lucky" one. The cops arrested him for possession of a concealed weapon without a permit and towed his motorcycle. Dee returned with the others to the operatives' undercover house where he received a phone call from Hells Angel member Martinez who was stranded at a nearby Denny's and needed a ride. It was now two o'clock in the morning. Without protest Bird tossed Dee the keys to his Mercury Cougar and, predictably, within an hour Dee returned to the residence with Martinez in tow.

At three o'clock in the morning, Martinez cut lines of meth on a dinner plate in the kitchen and snorted the dope with Dee. Pops slipped the leftovers to Bird who stashed the meth in a back closet for safekeeping. Just before dawn Martinez unloaded his arsenal of automatic weapons in the living room and spent the next few hours in a meth-induced stupor, obsessing over his physical appearance and stroking his goatee over and over again.

Unfortunately, Martinez wasn't the last houseguest the operatives had. Dee's prospect showed up the next day, released on bond and only mildly perturbed that he would have to return to court in ten days. Dee also became a regular in the weeks before Christmas. Bird worried that the team might crack under the strain of role playing 24/7. They were all exhausted . . . cloudy thoughts led to slipups and inconsistencies, none of which any of them could afford.

Bird worried especially about Pops's stamina. His nightmares aside, Pops had other concerns—he'd learned of the Hells Angels "snitch list." Among the walking dead was a female informant who was also a regular customer at the Inferno Lounge. Chef had somehow obtained paperwork from the Las Vegas Metropolitan Police Department that contained a photocopy of the woman's driver's license and her cooperation agreement. Pops recognized her; days earlier, she too had also partied at Smitty's.

INSIDE OUT

"I need your advice," Bird began over the telephone, hoping to massage Mesa Bob's ego by asking for his help in paring down Bird's prospecting choices, but the biker was in no mood for flattery. His tone was chilly and reserved as he dropped his bomb.

"What do you hear about Rudy?"

The question was a punch to the gut. Bob knew something. Bird swallowed, his lips parched. If he answered incorrectly, the entire investigation was over. *What had Bob heard?* More importantly, *whom* had he heard it from?

"I'd like us to meet," Bob replied. "Now, if possible."

"I'm in Nogales," Bird lied, stalling for time, his mind racing with questions. Rudy had a cooperation agreement with ATF and the United States Attorney's Office; in exchange for his assistance in Operation Black Biscuit, Rudy would receive a reduced prison sentence. What if things had gone awry and Rudy disclosed more than he should have to the wrong parties?

"When you return then," Bob relented, adding that his "prison sources" reported that Rudy was "talking too much."

Beef ordered an immediate debriefing of Rudy and learned that the CI had been solicited by an Aryan Brotherhood prison gang member and an inmate named "Trashcan" to commit a murder on behalf of Hells Angel

73

chapter member Howard Weisbrod (aka "Howie"), who was also wanted for the decapitation of the Mesa clubhouse woman. But that wasn't the worst of it. Apparently, Rudy had also bragged that the Solos planned to "patch swap" with the Hells Angels.

Mesa Bob stabbed at his breakfast as he discussed the development with Bird the following day at a Waffle House in Mesa. "He's not a snitch, but he's causing problems . . . if he's cooperating with the government . . . " Bad Bob finished his thought by jamming a square of waffle into his mouth.

They made an odd pair—the Hells Angel dressed in business attire, having just completed a sales training with Earnhardt Ford, and Bird looking like a pile of dirty clothes. Bird found it disturbing that Bob functioned on the "outside," that he lived a double life, interacted with regular folks on a daily basis, sat behind a wide-lipped desk in the dealership, and punched numbers into a computer to finalize car deals. Still, Bird supposed it made sense that Mesa Bob chose sales as his cover. Like Bird, Bob stayed as close to the truth as possible. After all, Bob was used to trafficking in arms and drugs. Cars weren't such a stretch.

Bird struggled to focus as he downed his fourth cup of coffee. *You're not like him. You're nothing remotely like him,* he insisted to himself.

The biker stuffed another cube of dough into his mouth and assured Bird that Rudy's indiscretions "would not reflect negatively on the Solos." His charter was still interested in recruiting Bird and his team as prospects. In fact Mesa Bob planned to discuss the issue at the next Arizona officer's meeting. If all went well, the Hells Angel leaned forward and winked at Bird, he would have some suggestions for Bird regarding the murder solicitation. He also promised to "counsel" the person who owned the firearm Rudy possessed when he was arrested; Mesa Bob would make sure that this person clarified for Rudy's attorney whose weapon it really was. The chapter president vowed that he had ways of handling situations, and that once Rudy's cooperation issue was taken care of, things would open up for the Solo Angeles.

"I've hung my ass out for you guys," Bob reminded Bird, waving a sticky fork in the air. "I'm responsible for the Solo Angeles presence in

Arizona. I've vouched for you guys to all the Hells Angels members I know."
Mesa Bob's concession was huge. He had never before sanctioned a new
club's desire to fly colors in the area. But he liked the Solos. He liked Bird.

Mesa Bob again leaned across the table, syrup glistening on his lower
lip and revealed, "I've said things to you that I haven't even told my clos-
est associate."

Bird absorbed the biker's monologue, his heart ticking like a small
bomb. They were so close . . . *Fucking Rudy,* Bird cursed. It didn't matter
that Rudy had been "officially" removed from the case, the CI was still a
threat to the operation. For the first time Bird's interests aligned with Mesa
Bob's—they both wanted Rudy "handled."

"We need to speed things up," Bird emphasized at the next Black Biscuit meeting. Beef paced the warehouse, his face flushed with tension. He
had promised the operatives reinforcements, but so far none had materi-
alized. Nobody blamed Beef. Not really. ATF suits were wary of wasting
human and financial resources on a mission accomplished. Maybe the
suits had a point, Beef reasoned. After all, wasn't it enough that the Pumpkins had convinced the Hells Angels that they *were* Solo Angeles or that
the Hells Angels had recruited them to prospect for club membership?

Bird scanned the exhausted faces of his team and knew the answer was
a resounding "no." They had each paid a high price to be there, and despite their waning morale, Bird was fairly certain none of them was leaving without huge consequences—indictments and lasting repercussions.

Bird chewed on a toothpick suddenly resenting Beef's perspective—
behind the scenes, shuffling papers, pacifying egos, playing the puppet
master. On his worst day Beef nursed a paper cut. Not fair.

The pair actually shared a healthy friendship, and as contentious as
Beef was, Bird never questioned his loyalty to or compassion for the team
or the operation. The Pumpkins were Beef's responsibility. He had recruited the players and he would damn well deliver them. He had to. How
else would his story be told? Beef had already assembled his fantasy cast of
Hollywood actors in *Black Biscuit—The Movie.* Beef, of course, had cast
Tom Berringer to do the honors and "Bennie" (the mentally handicapped
clerk from *L.A. Law* television series) to play the role of Bird. Levity
helped, but not everyone appreciated Beef's humor.

Buddha sat thoughtfully in a corner, stroking the mascot dragon lizard that was asleep on his shoulder. "We can't exactly speed things up with *three* people," Timmy complained, spilling hot coffee on his lap.

"Fuck you," JJ said, deflecting his insult. She coiled a strand of hair around her thumb and said nothing, her usual cheery self subdued. Perhaps she had seen too much or sensed the dark pull of fear that grips those who work deep cover when they realize they are truly alone and there will be no rescue.

Pops looked wan, paler than usual. In the span of two days, he had deftly negotiated gun deals and drug deals with Hells Angels members in Bullhead City, Kingman, and Tucson *and* had received yet another invitation to prospect. Joby, a Hells Angel Skull Valley member, had courted Pops at a truck stop in Kingman, eager to set up a date soon with the Solos to introduce them to his club members.

Bird worried that ATF suits might misinterpret the strategy of the operatives for hesitation, even fear. And he knew sooner or later the Hells Angels would call his bluff—he *talked* about club members, but he never produced any fresh faces.

"The brass is getting nervous," Beef confirmed. "They want to know what we're doing." He paused, hands on his hips, and uttered the words everyone dreaded, "They've threatened to shut the investigation down."

Pressure mounted. The operatives had no choice but to push forward and produce results. So far their investigation had more firmly established that the Hells Angels were a drug cartel that also trafficked in stolen property and illegal weapons and planned to mount a large-scale war against another motorcycle gang, the Mongols. Evidently, ATF wanted something sexier: homicide, the violent trademark of motorcycle gangs. The operatives needed to identify suspects in two murder investigations: the Laughlin casino shootout between the Mongols and the Hells Angels and the prison-gang-style decapitation of Cynthia Garcia, the Mesa woman who had "disrespected" the club.

On a frigid January morning, the team found themselves trapped in the guest home of a Tucson charter hang-around member, Danny Boy, and the husband and wife pair, Speedy and Barbara, negotiating for an eight ball of meth. Bird was numb as the trio bragged about being convicted felons in possession of sawed-off shotguns, proud that they regularly "distributed" narcotics while armed.

Bird absorbed the scene as if detached from his body. It was the only way he could process the distortions—the shapes that moved in the living room like one-dimensional creatures in a carnival fun mirror, elongating, shrinking. Their inane chatter swirled around Bird, interrupted only by the cry of an infant, buried amidst roaches and old pizza slices fringed with blue mold, over the baby monitor.

"Your baby needs you," Pops interrupted.

Danny Boy nodded, left the baggies of meth on the floor, and returned a few minutes later cradling a newborn in his arms.

"You want to do a line before you leave?"

Later that same night, in what would prove to be a turning point in the investigation, the operatives were invited to yet another Mesa clubhouse party. It was close to midnight when Bird and his exhausted team slid onto bar stools and watched with detached fascination as two bullish-looking Hells Angels members named Mutt and Pimp casually snorted meth off the edge of a knife and offered Timmy a line. Bird tensed, caught off guard by the gesture, suddenly keenly aware that theirs wasn't mere invitation but challenge almost as if . . . he quickly dismissed the thought.

There's no way they know you're a cop.

Still, Bird caught the glint of Mutt's Smith & Wesson pistol openly displayed on the Hells Angels' hip and wasn't so sure. He had heard the Hells Angels had allies inside the Mesa and Bullhead City police departments, dirty cops who wouldn't hesitate to tip off a member. His mind raced to Rudy—had the CI blabbed too much? Had a prison guard overheard? Timmy bristled, shifted uncomfortably on his stool. Bird resisted the urge to intervene. Like animals, the Hells Angels sensed weakness and wouldn't hesitate to put a bullet in Timmy's head. And hunt down his family for good measure. *Quick answer,* Bird telegraphed, *no hesitation, no pauses.*

"I have business in the morning," Timmy bluffed. Weak. Bird inwardly flinched.

"Then you'll just do it really fast," Mutt cocked his head to the side and pushed the knife closer.

"Save it for me," Timmy managed.

Bird forgot to breathe. He watched a muscle in Mutt's jaw tick as he sized up his prey, his expression feral. *It's over*, thought Bird. Emergency or not, Bird wasn't sure Timmy could pull it off. The detective had already had enough trouble battling extreme temperatures let alone the side effects of dope. Could he do it . . . *for the good of the cause?* Would he? Bird's heart pounded against his chest like so many fists against a door. They had to leave. Now. But before Bird could signal distress, Mutt smiled sardonically, nodded and poured a stash of meth into a ziplock baggie.

"Watch yourself leaving this place," Mutt warned.

But as the operatives stood to leave, Hells Angel member Calvin Schaefer, (aka "Cal") blocked their exit, and like dutiful servants, Mutt and Pimp slunk into the shadows. Cal, a skinny figure with a diamond goatee, ponytail, and tattoos on his throat that mimicked chain mail, had played a major role in the Laughlin Harrah's Casino shoot-out with the Mongols a few months earlier and was on the FBI's most wanted list. He would later claim it was "self-defense." He had heard that the Solos were involved in firearms trafficking, one of his specialties. Cal wanted to discuss business in private, at the Solos' residence. He leaned an elbow on the bar, cracked his knuckles, and noted that certain Hells Angels members had "hoarded" the operatives. He disliked exclusivity.

There were splinter groups within the Hells Angels who considered themselves renegades, part of the old-school culture that took care of business with violence. They were wild cards, unpredictable and reckless, dangerous to the status quo because they invited scrutiny through their criminal exploits and drug ingestion and threatened to ruin the public persona as misunderstood bikers who supported charitable organizations that the Hells Angels had worked hard to establish.

Cal pressed his head to Bird's and whispered conspiratorially, "Not everyone gets along with each other. Some of us, including myself, want to be *outlaws*."

WILD CARD

At dawn the next morning, Mutt and Cal roared up to the operatives' trailer on their Harleys dressed in full Hells Angels regalia and armed with semiautomatic firearms. Timmy ushered them inside and offered them an arm of ripped checkered sofa. But Mutt and Cal weren't interested in comfort; they were there to do business. Without mincing words they discussed the "items coming up from Mexico." But there was something odd about their hushed exchange. Bird shivered, his internal radar registering Cal's coded language, his frequent references to criminal exploits as "hypothetically speaking" as if he were building a defense in case Bird's fears were founded and Cal suspected the operatives were cops, or worse, snitches working for cops.

Bird digested the revelation slowly . . . they were being set up . . . he watched Mutt's eyes flick to the ceiling, to the walls, to any place that might conceal a camera or a listening device.

"We'd like to go slow," Cal advised. "We don't want Bob to know of our business with you," he continued.

Mutt grinned adding, "We just want to make money without taking legitimate employment."

He simulated a handgun and winked at Timmy.

Bird considered Cal's proposition to shun the status quo, defy Mesa Bob, and become an "outlaw" with measured reserve; he wasn't certain whether Cal wanted to do business with the operatives or eliminate them as competition. But Bird suspected flattery wasn't Cal's motive. The "outlaw" wanted to form alliances with Bird, Mesa Bob's strongest prospect, *recruit* him to his side in order to cripple Bob's leadership. Cal had tipped his hand—he considered Bird to be an outlaw of stature.

It was after midnight when Bird, Pops, Timmy, and JJ dragged themselves into the Mesa clubhouse bar, greeted by Cal and Jarhead, a self-described officer in the Mesa chapter. Pimp, whom Cal identified as "one of the five outlaws," slipped behind the bar and advised that he "had to stay straight tonight" because he "was working security." While Cal and Bird conversed, Pimp produced a slingshot and ball bearings that he used to shoot at the "pole camera" across the street and at unmarked police cars that happened to drive by.

"I've broken some windows," Pimp bragged.

Cal advised that the club was "security conscious" and that Mesa Bob was "paranoid," often using binoculars to perform countersurveillance.

"We're always being watched," Cal said. "And abused," he insinuated, describing how police routinely conducted felony traffic stops on members and failed to report hit and runs where members sustained injuries. The Hells Angels weren't really *people*; the group was a virus that had to run its course. And if the cops didn't quite follow protocol, who would know? More importantly, who would care? Bird felt suddenly small in the smoky space—one lone soldier amidst an enemy swarm—outnumbered but not outsmarted.

JJ meanwhile was a light that attracted moths: Cal's girlfriend, Sara, and Sara's cousin, KC. They fluttered around JJ, exchanged phone numbers like excited teenagers, discussed relationship problems, and negotiated drug deals. JJ became their confidante, dolling out advice, deflecting offers for dope by deferring to Bird; "He doesn't like it when I use the stuff, but I'll take a teener to take back to friends in San Diego," she compromised as if such conversations were normal. KC nodded, understood "the Solo Angeles business," and wanted JJ to relay to Bird that KC "could help them by running things south."

KC confided that she regularly transported narcotics between Phoenix and Los Angeles and bragged that her methamphetamine was "all chunk and crystal, no powder." KC had earned the Hells Angels trust; "they know I'll never rat them out," she bragged. "They paid off a judge in Los Angeles and my felony charges were dropped."

JJ promised to discuss KC's proposition with the club, maybe the next day at an organized Solo Angeles barbeque?

It was nearly dawn when the operatives arrived at headquarters for their nightly debriefing, but as exhausted as the team was, Beef insisted on a game of poker. He was unusually pumped, his face flushed with excitement. Bird thought Beef might implode as he snapped his fingers at Buddha and barked, "Get the chips." Beef rubbed his palms together and, like a giddy teenager, announced that he'd found the team five "aces"—experienced deep-cover ATF agents to play the missing Solos. The men were on loan for two weeks, borrowed from field divisions in Ohio, Montana, Mississippi, and San Diego to reprise their roles as hard-core bikers.

Their timing perfectly coincided with the Hells Angels annual Florence Prison Motorcycle Run in honor of biker "brothers behind bars." The Solo reinforcements represented a strong, united front to the Hells Angels.

Beef ordered the new recruits to blend, mix, and deflect attention. No one asked Beef for details. It was enough for the Pumpkins that their mascot had produced extra bodies they could parade around the Hells Angels and bolster their team's legitimacy as outlaw bikers.

"Take 'em around town and show them the sights," Beef said as he dealt the cards, straddled his chair backward, and winked at Bird.

Strip clubs, biker bars, and beer fests.

Bird had two weeks to expose the agents to as many Hells Angels members as he could find and sell the bikers a convincing story: the phantom Solos had kept a low profile ever mindful of Hells Angel protocol. "No one flies his colors in this state without my permission," Mesa Bob had frequently warned Bird.

Relief rippled through Bird as the agents introduced themselves. Their worn faces, heavily tattooed flesh, unkempt hair, and perfectly windburned cheeks lent credibility to their roles. And it helped that two of them were Hispanic. None required special coddling. In fact, less than

twenty-four hours after playing poker with the team, the Hells Angels insisted Bird "bring by his new dudes" to the clubhouse. To Bird's surprise
the invitation was a reprimand. The Hells Angels were actually miffed that
Bird had not thought enough of his relationship with the bikers to introduce the Solos to them immediately.

It was brilliant.

Bird played on Mesa Bob's wounded ego by extending to him a special
invitation. Never mind that Hells Angels as a rule did not support other
bikers, Bird insisted that it would be an honor if the Hells Angels dropped
by the next day to witness a patching-in ceremony. The team barely had
time to coordinate their cover stories. The most any of them knew was
that Sonny, as the youngest ATF recruit, would play the Solo prospect and
Steve, the other ATF agent, would play his sponsor.

The following afternoon, Timmy flipped steaks on the grill in the front
yard of the operatives' undercover home as nearly fifteen Hells Angels
members, including Mesa Bob, and their respective female companions
arrived in tandem on their motorcycles and parked in the street in an impressive display of metal and chrome. The fact that Mesa Bob came at all
was testament enough that he respected the Solos, that he also invited a
representative from each charter was a huge victory for the operatives. The
day was overcast and chilly—in direct contrast to the operatives upbeat
mood. A barbeque on monitored turf was just the social event the Pumpkins needed to flex their muscle.

They had a *team* now. A *club*.

They were less likely to get killed.

The promise of beer, arms, and dope was lure enough for the Hells Angels, but watching a prospect "patch in" to a club was an *event* and an
honor for the Hells Angels to witness. In a rare role reversal, the Hells Angels were the "special guests" of the Solos.

Bird set the stage for Sonny to receive his center membership patch,
marking him as a bona fide Solo Angeles, scripting the scene carefully,
mentally preparing for his own ceremony when he "made it" as a Hells
Angel. "Patching in" to the Hells Angels more often than not involved

ritual rites of passage: murdering for the club, excessive dope ingestion, unusual sexual acts, and displays of courage, "like putting a gun to a guy's head and pulling the trigger on a blank," Mesa Bob explained.

Sonny's story, while less dramatic, was nonetheless noteworthy: he had smuggled arms south of the border and supplied the Solos with a load of cash, which Bird now accused Sonny of pocketing. In an impressive display of acting, the operatives pretended Sonny was there to be eliminated. Timmy egged Bird on as Bird swore at Sonny, swung his baseball bat into a large rock that was supposed to simulate Sonny's head, and shouted, "You want a piece of this, prospect?"

Bird paused, bat in midair, and then, as if reaching under his colors for a gun, he pulled out the coveted top Solo rocker instead and threw it at Sonny. The crowd roared with approval, circled the agent, and sprayed him with beer until he was soaked. Cheers erupted as Sonny was lifted into the air like a star football player who had just scored the winning touchdown. The air was jubilant—filled with screams, laughter, and relief. The Solos had pulled off another ruse, another flawless performance for an audience of drunken fools.

While the team's confidence soared, Bird kept his enthusiasm in check, always reminded that the Hells Angels were a brutal and unpredictable group. His body shook with adrenaline and nerves as alternative deadly scenarios played in his head. One false move and it would have been over . . . for all of them. Paranoia gave way to giddy laughter as he acknowledged his team with a toast and a photo opportunity. Bird knew that they had all endured their own rite of passage and "patched in" to a world from which none would leave unscathed. As Bird draped his arms around his new recruits, unease rippled through him. Nerves betrayed ATF agent's Steve's face, flushed raw like rare meat. Sonny blinked beer from his eyes swept into a blessed dizzy moment of unconsciousness. Timmy's unkempt beard mercifully hid the quiver in his lower lip, and JJ's eyes were glossy like a deer that knows it's just dodged a bullet.

Pops wavered on the periphery, a ghostly old soul, and Bird wondered how the CI could stand it? *Maybe the way you do?* Bird's conscience nagged. Like it or not, the operatives had all passed the point of no return.

★ ★ ★

Even if Bird and his team walked away right now, they could never go back to a normal life, to a *recognized* life. They looked forward to living with shadows—phantom or real figures who stalked the corners of their everyday lives, waiting to expose them, murder them, or worse, ignore them. Deep cover was a thankless existence. Like Pops, Bird could perpetuate an identity in the underworld, glean satisfaction in deception, and be an unknown soldier, a hero.

Bird resigned himself to the life he chose and to the secrets he buried. He was never destined to shuffle papers at ATF. He felt enormous pride as he scanned his team—they had all sacrificed to be there. For Pops it was about redemption and doing something purposeful with what life remained. And even though he was on a government leash and there to do Bird's bidding, Bird liked to believe that Pops wanted to leave this world with a different legacy. He was more than a criminal and an addict. Black Biscuit had taken its toll on all of them, Pops included. Nonetheless the operatives persevered for the good of the cause, despite Beef's grumbling and the concern of the ATF suits that the operation had become too dangerous.

The patching in of Sonny had earned Bird instant respect among the Hells Angels, particularly Cal, who, with a mouthful of hamburger, casually divulged to Bird his involvement in the Harrah's Laughlin Casino shootout. Whether his confession was pure hyperbole or truth one thing was clear—he wanted to impress Bird. "I like the way you run your club," Cal remarked, nodding toward Timmy, who made a point to display his mock collection of illegal firearms to Mutt. "You understand that the most important issue is money." Cal's reference was meant as an insult to Bob, who had privately confided to Bird that he'd had to "reel in some of the members because they were getting out there."

Cal's excessive drug use had become a control issue for the motorcycle club. The rebel habitually missed "church," failed to "check in" with Bob, or reveal his activities. "I run a tight ship," Bob reminded Bird, as if the two shared a common bond. "Nothing moves in this town without me knowing about it." His eyes darkened as he spoke of Cal, who, like Rudy, had become a wild card for the club, or perhaps more pointedly, an ugly reminder that Mesa Bob, too, wrestled with the same demon that had *made* Cal a wild card: methamphetamines.

Bird watched Bob slip into a back bedroom of the operatives' trailer and nasally ingest the speed, his body shivering with the instant rush of dope. Moments later, Bob lit a marijuana cigarette, and, acknowledging Bird in the doorway, shrugged, "Mind if I smoke inside? It helps me settle down from the meth."

THE FLORENCE PRISON RUN

FEBRUARY 2003
The next few days were a blur of drug and arms deals as Bird introduced the new agents to the Hells Angels and to the exhausting pace of deep-cover work. Negotiations with transactions occurred sometimes at three and four o'clock in the morning in smelly cars, deserted parking lots, and at the operatives' own undercover residence. It was early February.

Tension bit through the chilly night air as Bird and his team arrived at the Hells Angels Cave Creek clubhouse. Bird sensed transition—acceptance into the old-school Hells Angels. Legends like Ralph "Sonny" Barger and Johnny Angel welcomed the Pumpkins inside their dumpy, unimpressive quarters, slapped them on the back, and ushered them into dark holes like rats. Intrigued by Bird's reputation as a "trafficker," members solicited him for "silencers" and "guns that go fast."

Johnny Angel meanwhile whisked ATF operative "Big Al" into a private room for a "history lesson" about the old-school Hells Angels. Angel was a commanding presence, a veteran member who boasted of at least forty-three years of loyalty to the club and allegiance to the Russian Mafia. The old biker sported two silver Death Head pins that signified his involvement with the Bones Motorcycle Club in Germany and Austria. Apparently, he'd traveled with ease throughout Europe, deftly handling the inquiries of custom agents at the borders. Those were "the good old days," Angel advised. Now the activities of club members revolved around methamphetamine. Where once Angel had recommended the Hells Angels consume no more dope than filled the "tip of a knife blade," club members now "were using big lines."

It was a different Hells Angels.

Violent, unorganized, and fractured.

The club hummed with white noise. The Florence Prison Run was scheduled to occur the next morning, and the members were giddy with anticipation, practically salivating beer as they gushed about motorcycle parts, repairs, and their Harleys. Riding was about power, flexing muscle, and commanding a formidable presence on the road. In a roar of support for their brothers behind bars, the Hells Angels made the annual 75-mile trek to Florence, a dusty old town whose prison housed some of Arizona's worst offenders. For a nominal donation to the defense fund, any club could participate. Members were encouraged to correspond with their prison brothers, their "Big House Crew" (BHC), and even circulate a "Big House News Letter," which contained a list of Hells Angels members in prison worldwide.

Inwardly, Bird cringed at the prospect of his team riding such a distance on precarious government bikes in desperate need of repairs. With hundreds of bikers surrounding them, the Solos were painfully outnumbered. If anything went awry, even with all of the surveillance and back-up support tailing them, the operatives would lose a firefight. The risks were high. But there were no options. They were supposed to be *bikers*. The Florence Prison Run offered them a humbling perspective—for the first time the idea of "ridin' free" was terrifying. Nothing, absolutely nothing, could go wrong.

The Pumpkins had grown accustomed to transporting their motorcycles in the bed of a surveillance trailer, only to unload them near their destination, smear the bikes with dirt and grease, and fake the look of a hard ride. It wasn't unusual for the Hells Angels to travel several hundred miles in a single day, spanning the distance from Tucson to Kingman to score a dope deal. The trailers not only provided necessary respite for the operatives as they struggled to maintain the harried pace of trafficking, but they also reduced the team's liability.

ATF didn't need more reasons to shut down the operation—the specter of injury, accident, or equipment failure only fueled the controversy surrounding Black Biscuit. "All it takes is one fuck-up," Beef mimicked Gordon, thumbs tucked under his armpits, his ugly mug contorted in a scowl.

Perhaps Beef should have clarified his "joking" remark. After all there had been *many* close calls with the trailer. Bird was not a "live to ride" kind of guy. In fact he had never owned a motorcycle and didn't even enjoy riding one. Riding was a necessary chore. Pack riding required full concentration.

When the Hells Angels ordered Bird and the boys to attend a run anywhere outside the immediate area, the trailer was used. Bird always concocted a story that he had a debt collection or a gun deal to do in the targeted area, and he would negotiate to meet the bikers at the run site. Either Timmy or JJ would then drive the truck, towing the motorcycles and trailers behind. Bird would arrive a few miles away, sometimes roused from sleep, only to put on his biker costume: boots, belt, jacket, vest. Then he would lie on the ground, wiggle and roll in the dirt, and mount up. Sometimes he'd take grease from the engine and smear it on his face and hands. Often he'd arrive to the site and his engine wouldn't even be warmed up.

The fact that the Hells Angels never caught Bird towing his motorcycle was a combination of luck and resourcefulness. Once the truck was involved in an unexpected collision on I-17 and the trailer was totaled. Bird worked like a crazed mechanic to fix the damage. But it was no use. For a few anxious moments, Bird grappled with the fear of exposure—any Good Samaritan could have pulled over to assist, cop or Hells Angel—and blown Bird's cover. It was an unspoken rule in deep-cover work—survival meant trusting no one, not even a cop. Although his team had been unable to confirm the Hells Angels "inside sources," it was assumed that the bikers had bribed law enforcement and planted informants. If Bird divulged his true identity to anyone, including a cop, he guaranteed his suicide.

Considering their predicament, JJ, in typical irreverent fashion, resorted to humor. Hands on her hips, head cocked to one side, she teased, "Jesus Christ, you might actually have to *ride* your motorcycle." Bird formed a mental image—*the Bitch fell off*—and tempered his irritation.

Trailers were not an option for the Florence Prison Run although the biker women and prospects generally followed the bikers in crash trucks (or war wagons). These vehicles, which ranged from vans to school buses, carried supplies—spare motorcycle parts in case of breakdowns, sleeping bags, beer, drugs, weapons, cell phones, and police scanners. The Solos were expected to ride at the front of the pack immediately behind the Hells Angels. Position mattered. *Protocol* mattered. The Solos were favored, respected, but most of all *trusted*. The operatives were more than a team now. They were a force.

The plan was to meet members of the Mesa charter at the Eagles Nest Lounge and follow them to the run site in Florence. Beer flowed as the outlaws gassed up, made last-minute repairs to their Harleys, and gathered like a swarm in the restaurant parking lot. Idle chatter reached a feverish pitch over the roar of engines. Exhaust filled the frigid air. Adrenaline pumped through Bird's veins as he straddled his bike with JJ clutched to his waist. The Solos had spent a sleepless night at the Black Biscuit warehouse, debriefing with Beef, lodging dope evidence, and tinkering with bike repairs. Beef had armed them each with tools—wrenches and tire putty, and like a good puppet master, he had sent them off to play.

Punctuality was not a strength of the Hells Angels. Nearly an hour after their scheduled departure time, the outlaws mounted their bikes, and in a belch of smoke and fuel, they maneuvered their metal beasts through Mesa's main streets and onto the open highway. Dressed in full-patched biker regalia, the outlaws formed an ominous presence, transformed from their daily lives as pilots and businessmen to devils. They traveled seamlessly, veering off the highway and onto dusty switchbacks, surrounded by red-tipped mountains. Florence was a town that smelled of another era—diners and grease and deep fried eggs. An old dead-end farm culture that existed the way Purgatory must—a way station for criminals and Hells Angels. A pack of outlaws banging clubs at the prison gates was a grim reminder to the caged "brothers" that there really *was* no escape.

Not for any of them.

Relief soured in Bird's mouth—his team may have survived the run without mishap, but in truth they were no better off than the inmates. There was a strange comfort in familiarity, and Bird too would gravitate to the danger he knew rather than adjust to the world he'd left. That was the "curse." While Bird fantasized at times about returning to the "outside" world, he also recognized the potential pitfalls. Like a soldier who transitions from war to civilian life, Bird's return promised to be as equally disorienting. Part of him longed for the sameness of everyday life, the other part of him thrived on the adrenaline undercover work delivered.

Pops was a good mirror for things to come: his ghostly visitations aside, he already suffered post-traumatic stress disorder and had to inhabit different worlds to cope. The old CI squinted at Bird, the bright sun beating down on his peppered ponytail. His face was windburned and flushed, his scarf little more than a decorative square of cloth. *He* had never escaped. And Timmy looked painfully cold, worn already by the day's events. Even an hour of sleep would do him well. Only the reinforcements bubbled with enthusiasm, tickled to be part of the operation and caught up in the energy of a *real* motorcycle run.

ACT II
INSIDE ANGEL

CLOSE CALL

Valentine's Day was sobering for Bird. Nearly one year had passed since the formation of the mock Solo Angeles, and the operatives were still deciding which Hells Angels charter to prospect. ATF brass was losing faith in Black Biscuit's goal. Some suits worried that the Pumpkins actually enjoyed playing outlaws and were too absorbed in the biker culture to differentiate the enemy.

Although he'd had several offers to prospect, Bird declined the invitations for a number of reasons: Strategically and logistically the mission couldn't afford to have the operatives divided among clubs, and no one charter was willing to sponsor all of them as a unit. More importantly, the charter Bird chose had to be fairly new, rogue, and willing to bend some rules. The more established quarters like Mesa and Tucson promised to keep Bird and his team as prospects for at least one year, a tenure that would not only cripple the operation but also guarantee attrition.

If the charter was small and desperate enough for members, Bird and his team could muscle their way inside and convince the Hells Angels to speed up the process. The objective of Black Biscuit was to infiltrate the club, not merely to engage the Hells Angels on the periphery. As Solo Angeles the operatives were limited in the intelligence they could gather. The Skull Valley charter was promising because of its size and members . . . but Bird needed an invitation.

Bird arrived at the Desperados Bar in Prescott with Timmy to attend
a support party for the Hells Angels Skull Valley charter. The reinforcements had already returned to their respective divisions after the operatives convinced the Hells Angels that the members had returned to
Tijuana. The Solos had again dwindled to three. The smoky bar pulsed
with mariachi music. Beer pooled on the counter and floor. Salsa spices
made Bird's eyes smart. A blur of bikers from the Hells Angels, Red Devils, the Desert Road Riders, and the Vietnam Vets clustered around the
pool table. Some were already sloppy drunk; others were enthralled with
the local strippers who lunged at the bikers' cash like desperate hyenas
grateful for scraps. Bird winced at the scene, disturbed by the concept of
human property and powerless to stop the exploitation. As always,
women, like bike parts, were swapped at random.

There was an edge to the air, a strange heaviness that pricked the back
of Bird's neck as he and Timmy waded through the dirty patches of heat
to join Pops, who was already nursing a beer at the bar. The old CI resembled a dry cactus husk, brittle and pale, wise to the life Bird struggled
to endure. Bird ordered a beer, propped his elbows on the bar, and eyed
the bikers the way a hunter sizes up prey he intends to kill.

Hells Angel member Joby grunted his greeting to Bird and advised in
a low whisper that he had met with the firearm silencer manufacturer in
Bullhead City and "everything's a go."

Thumbs up.

Joby resembled more ape than human with his tufts of unkempt hair,
grizzly beard, and thick long arms that dragged against his stocky frame.
Joby leaned close, his words grazing the shell of Bird's ear. "Meet me in
private," he demanded.

Bird's heart raced as he followed Joby to the only quiet place in the bar,
the urinal. *Now what? Had Joby learned the truth about Bird? Had the biker
been ordered to "take care of business"?* It was never a good thing to be sin-
gled out and removed from public view. Panic zipped through Bird as he
envisioned Joby patting him down for a recording device and then calmly,
with his newly purchased silencer, putting a bullet in Bird's head.

Fear replaced reason as memories of Timmy's ordeal with Hank resur-
faced and the time Dee had cornered Bird in a bar in Mesa and engaged

him in animated discussion about hunting Mongols. That time, from Timmy's perspective at the counter, their heated exchange and wild hand gestures had signified trouble, "the shit was on," and Timmy very nearly pulled his weapon in defense. Judgment required skill and quiet calculation. Seemingly threatening demeanor from a Hells Angel could in fact be nothing more than passion, however misguided. Although the decision to wear a wire was always risky when gathering intelligence from the biker community, Bird needn't have worried about detection.

Protection from his back-up crew was something else entirely.

The wire was designed to record, not transmit conversations. As a result the surveillance team had to rely on observation and Bird's intermittent phone calls to report his status. If the operatives were ever in trouble, the crew's response would quite possibly be too late.

"We're your little pissants," Buddha complained once. "While you party your ass off every night drinking and smoking, we're stuck inside this stinking van waiting for something to happen."

"You want to trade places?" Bird challenged, ending Buddha's rant. The rivalry between the two factions was palpable.

"What's the plan?" Buddha whined at headquarters one night.

"The plan?" Bird quipped.

"Plan B," Buddha clarified. "You know . . . if you guys get in trouble?"

"We'll plow our van through the fucking walls," Beef supplied.

And he meant it. Beef really intended to ram his government-issued van, like a tank, into the nearest wall if things suddenly spun out of control.

The operatives had learned to steer clear of business fronts, favoring corners instead, bar counters, back, rooms and . . . , Bird sighed, urinals.

Since the nature of intelligence gathering was more improvisation than plan, Bird had learned to expect surprise.

Instinct guided him.

It was Bird's call.

He could end it now, retreat, summon his backup, and engage in a bloody brawl or . . . he could take a risk. A private huddle with Joby might yield a rare admission—Joby had ordered "prototypes" built for 9mm and .45 caliber firearms and promised to include a special for

Bird—incriminating conversation all recorded. It was hard enough to make a federal case against the Hells Angels, but without solid evidence like admissions of criminal activity, Bird's efforts would be wasted. As Bird moved toward the urinal, his gut clenched, he felt as if he were being pulled by an ocean current.

He barely remembered to breathe . . . If Timmy and Pops sensed he was in trouble and made a phone call or pulled their weapons, it was all over.

Joby likes you. Bird tried to convince himself that he really wasn't in as much danger as he felt he might be.

"I don't have to teach you how to be a Hells Angel," Joby complimented Bird, as the biker straddled a urinal in the men's bathroom and invited Bird to do the same. "You get it," Joby continued tapping a finger to his forehead. He paused, waited a breath, and said, "I want you to be my prospect."

The invitation to join the Mohave Valley charter signified a turning point in the Black Biscuit investigation. As a newly formed, exclusive charter with few members, Joby could afford to bend the rules to fill empty spaces. His bond with legendary Sonny Barger also gave him special privileges and he sweetened the invitation for Bird. "I could reduce the Solos hang-around time to just two days," he advised, "and you would only have to prospect for ninety . . . I know what you guys do for a living," Joby lowered his voice, alluding to Bird's debt collections and firearms trafficking. "I don't care," he assured, putting up a hand as if to ward off protest, "I don't expect accountability."

It was almost too perfect. The Solos could become members of the "Graveyard Crew" just like that *and* have the club's blessing to gather and report intelligence.

Mere devil's play.

It was after midnight when Bird, Timmy, and Pops arrived at the Mesa clubhouse for another evening of beer, conversation, and evidence gathering. The usual crowd greeted them—Crow, Trigger, Ghost, and Cal. Bird immediately approached Crow, intrigued by the firearm he habitually strapped to his shoulder. The worn Hells Angel towered over Bird, imposing and freakish. Like a crow, the biker had a tiny skinny head that bobbed on broad square shoulders. His chiseled features were marked by weathered skin the color of wet stone.

Crow ushered Bird to the bar, removed his Taurus 9mm semiautomatic pistol, and gave it to Bird to inspect. Timmy and Pops lingered behind. Casual banter had no effect on Crow. He was strictly about business. Bird offered to purchase Crow's gun for $400. The firearm had special meaning for Crow—the biker advised he had used it to commit a homicide, "I shot the bastard in the head at point blank range," Crow said matter-of-factly as if he were sharing a story about the weather. As confirmation of his kill, he pointed out blood spatter on the barrel and then, in a rare gesture of support for Bird, Crow removed the small knife he wore around his neck and gave it to Bird as a gift, "from one outlaw to another."

Crow sobered, cleared his throat, and confided to Bird that he was upset with Big Time Mike for disrespecting his wife. Big Time Mike was the owner of the Desert Flame Lounge, and Crow didn't appreciate the low wages his wife received for being his employee. "I'm going to kill him tomorrow night," Crow announced. His was a statement not a plan, and he needed Bird's help to flee to Mexico after he finished the deed.

Bird digested Crow's information slowly, a mixture of panic and nausea forming in his gut. Crow wasn't one for idle boasting. And Bird didn't have sufficient time to devise an effective strategy to thwart Crow's appetite for murder or convince him there were less drastic measures available to teach Big Time Mike a lesson. Bird couldn't exactly warn Big Time Mike to disappear either; Crow would know who had tipped him off and target Bird instead. Bird had little choice but to alert Beef and the surveillance team to Crow's intentions and insure that Crow never had a chance to carry out the execution of Big Time Mike.

Liver light filtered through the kitchen blinds in the undercover house, which was situated just one mile south of the Angels' Phoenix clubhouse. The Hot Headz, as they were sometimes called, had grown a little testy in recent weeks about the close proximity of the house to the turf of the Angels. But Beef wasn't concerned. Not yet.

Bird skinned potatoes, relishing the simplicity of the task. It was nearly dusk, and the operatives had hours before their next scheduled event with the Hells Angels. JJ and Timmy, enjoying a rare respite, lounged in the living room, their orange vests flung casually over chair backs, their boots tossed aside. JJ had completed her good deed for the night and fed scraps and ice cream to the stray neighborhood dogs. Now, relaxed in bare feet, ripped jeans, and T-shirt, she still wore her Sig Sauer strapped to her hip. No undercover was ever "off duty." She and Timmy engaged in spirited discussion about Black Biscuit in general and players in particular.

Bird tuned them out, too drained to participate. A familiar calm enveloped him like the strange quiet that consumes a house once full of children. Suddenly, he felt too large in the waning light, self-conscious when he spoke, unusually alert and painfully alone. Yesterday Crow revealed his murder plans to Bird, this morning Bird tossed a football with his son. He could *play* normal, but he could never *be* normal.

Bird put the knife down on the cutting board and reached into his pocket for his son's lucky rocks. One by one he ran them through the water, watching as their grey skin bruised black in the spray. The rocks were real. But even they could transform their appearance. Bird's mind was restless as he reviewed the week's events, worried that he might have slipped, let his guard down, and relied too much on the ATF reinforcements to perpetuate his identity. He had been without a team for so long . . . had the new agents sudden arrival and abrupt departure generated suspicion instead of confirmation that the Solos were a legitimate presence?

Bird had carried the lie alone for weeks after Carlos and Rudy were removed. As the token Hispanics it made sense to the Hells Angels that those two would handle the Mexican side of the gun-smuggling operation. Pops was a poor substitute, but so far he had pacified the Solo Angeles president, Suzuki, and paid his dues to the club in Tijuana. There had been no complaints. Still, the thought had to have occurred to the Angels that the Solos were unusual—a club of three members, none of whom was Mexican.

Instinctively, Bird sensed his time was short. He wiped the wet rocks with a paper towel and slipped them into his pocket. Nearly every charter in Arizona had invited him to prospect, and not just him, his whole team, including "the dudes who showed up for the Florence Prison Run," Joby insisted. The trouble was, none of the charters wanted all of them to prospect together for the same club.

The mere invitation to prospect for the Hells Angels signified that Black Biscuit was a success. Case over. They could all go home. The Hells Angels regarded the operatives as fellow outlaws, confided in them their dark ambitions—murder plots, quest for silencers, Mongol hunts. ATF had enough evidence against the Hells Angels to charge them with RICO[11], weapon and gun violations, drug and arms trafficking, and yet . . . Bird argued with Beef to keep the operation alive. He was so close. It wasn't enough for Bird and his team to become prospects.

Bird wanted to *be* a Hells Angel.

"You're jeopardizing lives because of your ego?" Beef challenged.

"Our mission was to infiltrate the Hells Angels," Bird reminded Beef.

"We have enough evidence," Beef countered.

We could get more as Hells Angels, Bird frowned, remembering his terse conversation with Beef. It wasn't ego, Bird insisted. It was the cause. He hadn't worked so hard to come this far just to quit. Instinctively, Bird knew that if he continued, ventured deeper into the organization, he would deliver murderers to ATF. If he could do that, Bird would not only destroy the public's perception of the Hells Angels as harmless renegade bikers who raised money each year for charities, but he also would cripple the criminal enterprise and send its leaders to prison for years.

Bird picked up his paring knife and began slicing potatoes again. Chatter buzzed around him like white noise interrupted only by the beep of Bird's pager. He glanced at the screen, his hands damp, full of vegetable skins: 911. He dropped the knife into the sink. It clattered against the ceramic. He didn't bother to turn off the faucet. The phone on the kitchen wall felt miles away. He motioned to the others to stop talking. Their faces froze in panic. Something had gone terribly wrong. Bird reached for the phone, his nerves shattered, his fingers thick and awkward on the keypad as he dialed Beef. A thousand scenarios raced through his mind.

"What's happened?" Bird's voice was tight, urgent.

"Get out," Beef ordered.

"What's going on?" Bird pressed.

---

[11] RICO, Racketeer-Influenced and Corrupt Organizations.

"Don't ask questions, just get out now!" Beef yelled. "They're coming over to kill you."

Bird dropped the phone, left it swinging on the cord. He drew his gun, put a finger to his lips, and motioned with his eyes for the others to follow him quietly out the back exit and into the street.

PATCHING UP

FEBRUARY 2003

The operatives were careful to leave separately and detour through back streets, frontage roads, and quiet, dilapidated neighborhoods as they rode to their debriefing at the warehouse. With his nerves shot Bird still remembered to shed his Solo Angeles identity before arrival at Black Biscuit's headquarters—all trappings were carefully concealed, disposed of, or otherwise stored prior to entering the Pumpkin Patch. Out of one skin and into another. Those were the rules, in case an agent picked up a tail, suspicious eyes, or even a curious street urchin. The warehouse was a safe haven, and it had to remain as such for the protection of the crew inside and the integrity of the operation.

Bird's mind raced with questions: *Where had he gone wrong? What little mistake had he made? Had Pops succumbed to his demons? Had Bird been too cavalier with Pops's post-traumatic stress? Or was there someone else, a rogue among the Hells Angels whose suspicions about Bird had been confirmed?*

Adrenaline propelled him around corners, his eyes darting from the road to the rearview mirror and to the shadowy houses that hugged the sidewalks like trolls. JJ's fingers gripped his waist betraying her nerves. She was young in this dark, what hard-edged persona she conveyed dropped away in that instant when Bird signaled them to leave. She didn't even take her boots.

Guilt wadded Bird's throat. Never mind that JJ had volunteered for this assignment. Did any of them really know what price they would pay? She was twenty-nine for Christ's sake. Her frame of reference stemmed from four years of college and drunken fraternity parties. And yet the Hells Angels had embraced her, and Bird had encouraged her to stay for selfish reasons. He needed a buffer, an excuse not to bed every crank whore the Hells Angels offered him. But JJ had surprised him. She was more than eye candy; her self-possessed demeanor, humor, and courage had propelled her . . . and *him* to a different status.

Without JJ, Black Biscuit might have ended much sooner.

As he steered his motorcycle to a dead-end road thick with cholla and prickly pear cactus, he removed his vest, folded it carefully into a square, and shoved it inside his saddlebag. JJ dismounted, and without a word walked barefoot along the dusty road; it was better to separate. Bird shoved his Sig Sauer into the rear of his waistband and put his bike in neutral so that he could coast it to the Pumpkin Patch—stealthy, inconspicuous. The motorcycle was merely a stage prop, disguised for different operations, recycled, and stored.

The streets were eerily empty . . . almost as if the families inside knew that blood was about to be shed.

Only the soft rustle of rack weeds blew around him.

Bird was certain Black Biscuit was over.

"What the hell happened?" Bird demanded once safe inside the Pumpkin Patch.

JJ lit five cigarettes in a row and stamped each one out on the metal table, watching the butts spark and whither to ash. "This is shit," she breathed, fear filling her lungs. Timmy sat quietly numb across from her, stirring his coffee with a pencil.

Beef stood at the head of the table, hands on his hips, looking drained.

"We need to pull out," he announced.

"Who's the snitch?" Bird demanded.

"An informant working for DEA as a Hells Angel prospect under Chico tipped off the DEA agent that Chico was assembling a hit squad of old-school Hells Angels, former Dirty Dozen members, to take out the Solos Angeles."

What the informant didn't know was that the Solos Angeles were cops. Fortunately for the operatives the DEA agent working the case knew about the ruse and immediately alerted Beef.

Mistake number one: Bird had dismissed Chico's turf complaints as petty. Although he knew the biker disliked him and had issues about the undercover house being situated within the jurisdiction of the Phoenix Hells Angels, he had no idea to what extent Chico might go, and he had never bothered to develop intelligence on him. Bird's focus had always been elsewhere.

Unwittingly, Bird had become a household name among the Hells Angels, attending so many sanctioned functions that he had become nationally renowned, even infamous, amidst certain circles. As it turned out, the San Diego Hells Angels fraternized with the Solo Angeles in Los Angeles and began to buzz about Bird's influence. Those who resented Bird's power began to demand answers. "Who the hell are these guys in Arizona?" "Fucking frauds," the rumors flew. "These assholes muscled their way into our club . . ."

Mistake number two: Bird should have been more aware. He never accounted for rogues.

Mistake number three: Bird enjoyed embellishing his exploits—real and imagined—partly out of arrogance but also out of need. After all, he had created his character, and like any good method actor, he filled in the details, bragging about his contract hits, gun running, and periodic meetings with Mafia types. He was larger than life, almost a cartoon. And yet, Mesa Bob had vouched for him, given him permission to fly his Solo colors in Arizona. With Bob's blessing Bird and his team had infiltrated the Hells Angels most sacred events and generated jealousy among charter members.

Mistake number four: Bird had been overconfident. He had been recruited by nearly every Hells Angel charter to prospect. He had played his part well, but even he knew there were holes in his story, gaps that should never have passed scrutiny.

For nearly a year Bird had mingled with the Hells Angels as part of a club of three, deflecting questions from the Hells Angels about his leadership skills, his fallen president, Carlos's departure (whom Mesa Bob vowed to "bring back in" to prospect), and his so-called Mexican roots. Why had he never traveled to Tijauna for instance to pacify Suzuki? Bird had used his cover as a gunrunner to excuse his absence, and he'd had no time to attend church with Suzuki. So he sent his minions—Rudy and Carlos at first, and now Pops. It made sense to Mesa Bob that the token Hispanics would "handle" their Mexican affairs. Pops raised a few eyebrows, but Bird squelched the skepticism by reminding the Hells Angels that Pops was a smuggler and an artful one. He was helping to arm his Solo brothers against the Mongols.

Chico's intended executions of the operatives had been thwarted . . . this time. Beef was adamant that there wasn't going to be a "next time." "It's over." He was emphatic. He had already begun to recite with his fingers the kinds of charges they had on the Hells Angels, what he was certain would bring indictments and convictions—RICO, drug and gun negotiations and purchases—small stuff, small consequences. The sad truth of the matter was that for all of their efforts, the Hells Angles were likely to walk away with probation, some jail, and maybe, if the operatives were lucky, prison.

Chico's threats did more than prompt Beef and ATF brass to want to shut down Black Biscuit; it also prompted Bird's allies to ask questions. Mesa Bob arranged a meeting with Bird, intimating over the phone that he "wasn't pleased" with the rumors that the Solos were frauds. While Bob assured Bird that he didn't accept the allegations outright, the "situation posed a serious problem." The Hells Angel had grown weary of bailing Bird out of fixes: Rudy's indiscretions, Carlos's departure, and the everdwindling members of the club. Bob announced that he'd grown "uncomfortable" with the few numbers; "you have only three guys," he pressed. Mesa Bob needed "assurances."

"Let's play this out," Bird suggested.

"Why, so he can finish what Chico started?" Beef challenged.

Bird couldn't blame Beef. The thought had crossed his mind as well that Mesa Bob accepted the rumors that the Solos were frauds and was preparing to execute him.

"I won't meet him without backup," Bird offered.

Beef nodded. "Watch yourself," he said.

Meanwhile, the Black Biscuit team prepared for a monumental shoot-out. Armed with sniper weapons, shields, helmets, and bulletproof vests, the crew was dressed in full SWAT regalia. Bird met Mesa Bob inside the Mesa clubhouse in the middle of a brisk afternoon. More alert than he'd ever been, Bird slid across from Bob and tried to look calm. Bob cracked his knuckles and circled his thumb around the rim of his beer stein, his eyes shifty and nervous. He was stalling. *Out with it already,* Bird telegraphed, glancing behind him, half expecting other Hells Angels to emerge from the cloudy darkness and open fire. Never mind that such a scenario made little sense. Bob wouldn't need to summon extras. He would do the deed himself in private and cover up his tracks.

Seconds ticked by. The only sound Bird heard was the hum of a television set flashing news bites in the lounge. The silence unnerved him. The Mesa clubhouse typically pulsed with managed chaos, clusters of bikers, some intoxicated, others high from methamphetamines. The place was never quiet. Not like this. Chatter generally filled the air like that of a flock of macaws. Bird paused, cleared his throat, and when he was certain he wasn't about to be the target of an ambush, he offered Bob the name of a Solo Angeles contact in Los Angeles, who would vouch for Bird's Arizona presence.

"Look him up," Bird challenged, confident that his ATF plant would perpetuate the ruse on the other end. Still unconvinced, Bird reminded Bob how they first met through Rudy, his numerous arms and drug deals, his reputation in Bullhead City, his team's trips to Tijuana to attend church and pay club dues.

"Sure there are guys that don't like us white boys in Arizona," Bird continued, careful not to show disrespect to Chico. "There're Hells Angels that don't like *you*." Bird licked his lower lip, waiting for Bob to process this information.

"I'm the real deal." Bird's voice went up an octave as he spread photographs of himself at a Solos Angeles party in San Diego sporting his biker cuts, a club photo of the Solo Angeles nomads, and the Solo Angeles' clubhouse in Tijuana. Bird even shoved a VHS newscast of himself posing with the Solo Angeles at a biker toy run in San Diego.

Bird reminded Bob of all the functions he had attended with Bob and the Hells Angels, "I've seen you ingest dope, negotiate drug and arms deals," Bird insisted, hoping he was as good a salesman as Bob. He had no choice but to convince Bob that he was legitimate—if he failed he was a dead man. Bob stood to lose face if he made the wrong call. After all, he had vouched for Bird's presence in Arizona, even authorized the club's permission to wear Solo Angeles colors in the state. If he was wrong about Bird . . . he wouldn't hesitate to take action "for the good of the cause."

Bird barely breathed, the muzzle of his gun cool against his back.

Bob nodded, grim-faced, and wagged a finger at Bird, "I believe you man," he said, and he rose to make a phone call. Without further questioning Bob advised that he "would take care" of the rumors marring the reputation of the Solo Angeles, "but you'll have to remove your colors until the problem is resolved. And you'll need to ditch that house too," Bob added, concerned that its location on the turf of the Angels had sparked Chico's suspicion.

"Give Mesa some thought," he suggested and placed a phone call to the president of the Phoenix charter. Bird listened in disbelief as Bob pacified the leader, advised him that he had the Solo Angeles problem under control, and that the Hot Headz should trust Bob's judgment as a twenty-three-year member. When he hung up the phone, Bob instructed Bird to "correct the political problem that led to the false information being passed to the Hells Angels." Meanwhile, Bob advised that he would like to meet the Solo Angeles who damaged Bird's reputation and "take care of business."

The next day was a flurry of activity for the Black Biscuit crew as members raced to vacate the undercover pad, remove sensitive cameras and bugs, and relocate the Pumpkins to a new safe house in Mesa. Bird, meanwhile, pacified Bob and assured him that any legitimacy issues concerning the Solos Angeles presence in Arizona had been alleviated; the club had the blessing of the Solos Angeles from the Los Angeles charter, and Bird produced physical evidence to support his position. Bob accepted the fake authorization documents supplied by ATF and promptly restored the permission to fly Solo Angeles club colors in Arizona.

But other Hells Angels were not so easily persuaded. The Bullhead City clan demanded further explanation from the Solos and also issued an ultimatum—either prospect for the Hells Angels now or suffer further scrutiny and consequences.

Bird accepted the challenge and traveled to Bullhead City with Timmy and JJ to discuss the particulars with Smitty at the Inferno Lounge. Bird had conditions. If he was to prospect for the charter, the Hells Angels would have to sanction his continued debt collections and firearms trafficking.

Seated across from Smitty, Bird shoveled a brown mass of Mexican food into his mouth and between slurps recounted the "Chico affair," dismissing the threat as misguided rivalry and jealous retaliation for Bird's influence. Smitty nodded, the gold chain around his neck disappearing into folds of skin. He and Joby had already discussed Bird's "needs"; accountability wasn't an issue. Competition was fierce between the charters, and if the operatives wanted their freedom, the Skull Valley charter was more than willing to oblige. The formation of a Hells Angel charter in Bullhead City was critical to the Hells Angels control of the region, Smitty advised.

Joby apparently had plans to form a "Bermuda Triangle"—a Hells Angel alliance between charters in Bullhead City, Las Vegas, Nevada, and San Bernardino, California. The operatives were integral to this plan, Smitty advised, and he intended to extend a solid recruitment offer to the Solos after the Fifty-fifth Anniversary Party in San Bernardino.

JJ had also unwittingly become part of "the old ladies" recruitment campaign. Most of these women were tweaker thin and aged like cheese, their youth swallowed in dope and smoke. They found great relief in terror and functioned as survivors do in that strange space between edge and abyss. Their safe haven was the biker world where they understood the rules and boundaries. No outsiders ever infiltrated their cocoon. And so their lives felt normal, deprogrammed, erased. They had no past and no escape. Being the old lady of a Hells Angel was a badge of honor and, sadly, gave the women purpose.

"Could you handle being with Bird if he becomes a member?" Lydia asked, sucking on a cigarette.

"Handle him?" JJ asked.

"It's not always easy being the old lady of a Hells Angel," Lydia warned, lowering her voice she added, "You'll need to pack heat, carry supplies—bulletproof vests, dope, guns . . . and hide their shit." Lydia spread her legs and pointed to her crotch.

"You're a good looker," Lydia continued as if that gave JJ special benefits. "No one will mess with you . . . unless Bird orders it of course."

"Good Lookers" enjoyed some prestige in the biker community because they guaranteed a steady source of income to the club; these women stripped in topless bars where they hustled drinks, prostituted themselves, or set up patrons for rips. Women like Lydia were valuable to the Hells Angels in other ways—they gathered intelligence and frequently worked as employees of telephone companies or secretaries in city, county, or state offices. Some even obtained positions in police records divisions.

JJ wasn't sure whether Lydia viewed her as a threat or an equal? As Bird's old lady, JJ belonged to him and accepted that, in the biker protocol, she would always be his last priority. A Hells Angel's first loyalty was to his club and to his brothers. His second priority was to his motorcycle. Dogs were third. Women were last.

FAST TRACK

As reassuring as it was for the operatives to have several Hells Angels charters vying for the Solos commitment to prospect, Bird was cautious, unconvinced that Chico's storm had passed. He wasn't about to make the same mistake twice. Instead Bird perpetuated his fake identity as a debt collector, preying on select Hells Angels members to assist him with particularly difficult clients. His ruse served a dual purpose: to thwart further club scrutiny and to promote reverence for the Solo Angeles.

Bird targeted Robert McKay, aka "Mac," a squatty troll-like Tucson Hells Angel member who owned the Rose Tattoo Parlor just blocks from the Tucson ATF headquarters building as a possible accomplice. Mac was prohibited from officially associating with the Hells Angels (i.e., other felons) due to his felony probation status. If caught by his probation officer, he could be violated and returned to prison. Worse, he would invite the cops and unwanted scrutiny of the Hells Angels. Still, it was hard for Mac to stay away from his brothers. He had resorted to disguises, wigs, and nose pieces when in their company.

Bird seized Mac's precarious status with the Hells Angels as an opportunity to manipulate the biker, to ply him for information, and to appeal to his wounded ego. Over the last several months, Bird had sacrificed his inner wrists to Mac's needle. Quick bursts of heat left a black-ridged sleeve along Bird's arms—a flesh shirt that would haunt him long after Black Biscuit ended. The branding was not only ritual and part of the biker culture, but it also established ownership among club members and made it nearly impossible to leave. Some Hells Angels had tattooed their entire chests with the trademark Death's Head and full-patch top and bottom rockers.

Bird made it a point to blend with the usual customers, arriving well after midnight so as to avoid detection and offering Mac wads of cash for his artwork. In exchange Bird hoped Mac would talk. Mac was a businessman and an opportunist, and Bird wasted little time soliciting the Hells Angel's help in recovering an outstanding debt. Bird hoped Mac would take the bait, participate in a deal, and report back to the Hells Angels that Bird's connections promised large profits for the club . . . and if Bird was valuable to the Hells Angels, the members might just relax the prospecting rules and expedite his status to full-patched member.

"The guy's a playboy," Bird explained, selling his upcoming collection to Mac. "He travels with bodyguards."

Mac grunted with interest as he dabbed Bird's bloody wrist with a cloth. Bird elaborated for the sake of the ruse and described in great detail his debt collection process, particularly why he thought Mac would make a great asset. The Rose Tattoo Parlor had the allure of a hair salon, holding patrons hostage for hours at a time while Mac chatted, inked, and gossiped. Bird counted on Mac to brag about his exploits with Bird. This was Mac's "big break" to launch a side career as a debt collector.

"I won't wear my vest," Mac whispered, "the club would never approve." The Hells Angels didn't help other biker clubs, but more importantly, Mac was on probation and the Hells Angels wouldn't want him to attract police attention. But Mac was willing to take a risk, and in an odd twist, go undercover for the Solos. He would assume the role of "Intimidator."

"JJ will lure the bastard to Tucson," Bird explained. "She'll bring him to the Waffle House for breakfast."

At noon Bird and Mac rode in tandem on their motorcycles to the restaurant. It was unusually warm for March. Hot wind whipped Bird's face as he rode the congested streets to the Waffle House, idling behind serious cyclists who did their best to ignore him and unsuspecting vans full of kids. Only the children stared at him through dirty back glass, unafraid, curious, as if he were a strange new zoo animal.

Mac followed closely behind, the chrome on his handlebars glinting in the bright sun. Daylight must have been a welcome change for the biker who lived most of his time like a roach in the dark. The Rose Tattoo Parlor was not only Mac's studio but also his home. Bird imagined Mac shuffling upstairs to collapse on an old dirty mattress, his head full of meth, his body twitching with fatigue. Like the other bikers Mac rarely slept, preferring instead to work and score business. Bird preyed on his need, often arriving at the parlor as late as 2:00 A.M.

Arriving at the restaurant, Mac backed his bike into a parking space in an effort to conceal his license plate. Bird smothered a smile, secretly pleased by Mac's paranoia. JJ sat at a corner booth with ATF Special Agent Whitley,[12] who played the target of the debt collection. Although Whitley was a veteran undercover agent, his role was limited but purposeful— he was to dress rich, speak little, and *look* like a playboy. No one said anything to him about being classy rich. Whitley dripped with gold jewelry and smelled of cheap hair gel. JJ caught Bird's eye as he and Mac waded through the after-church crowd, bickering families, and elderly couples happily silent.

Bird nodded at JJ and slid into the booth beside Whitley. As if on cue, Mac joined him. Whitley placed his fork down slowly and wiped syrup from his lower lip with his napkin. He made a point of scanning the restaurant parking lot for his fictitious bodyguards, and with a steely last glance at JJ, Whitley reached into his suit pocket and produced a checkbook, a wad of cash, and his Sig Sauer 9mm pistol. His moves were deliberate and resigned, as he wrote Bird a check for $17,000 and counted $300 in cash in front of Mac.

With exaggerated bravado Bird pocketed the money and gun and ordered Whitley to leave. Panic creased Mac's face as he grabbed Bird's arm, urging Bird to wait in the Waffle House until Whitley was gone; the biker couldn't risk detection or recognition. His license plate was turned toward the street, away from public's view, but still . . . Bird nodded, mentally applauding his victory as he paid Mac $200 for his assistance in the collection.

---

[12] Pseudonym.

Ninety percent of undercover work was showmanship and great story-telling. Bird hoped his latest efforts produced rave reviews with his fans. He needed more than damage control. He needed allies.

"See how easy it is," Bird said.

Later that day, JJ plied KC for methamphetamine, not for her she explained, but for Pops, who was road weary and headed home to Tucson. KC accepted the lie and agreed to meet JJ at Chopsticks, a Chinese restaurant in a seedy Tempe area. Secrecy was necessary, KC explained, because Mesa Bob had pulled Cal's patch, suddenly intolerant of Cal's drug addiction and KC's methamphetamine deals inside the clubhouse. Bob preached discretion. Image mattered. The Hells Angels needed to perpetuate their public repu-tation as a charitable band of misunderstood societal misfits. The truth—that the Hells Angels were involved in organized crime, money laundering, brutal killings, and dope and arms smuggling—could be bad for business.

The restaurant was nearly empty when JJ ordered black tea from the Mexican waitress who spoke only Spanish. The place smelled of boiled chicken. Red lanterns lit the ceiling. It was late and the owner, a slight eld-erly Caucasian man, swished a broom around her table. KC arrived in a puff of smoke, her old pickup truck in need of engine repairs. The tweaker twitched to JJ's table and slid across from her. In the dull red light, KC re-sembled a gutter rat, her thin pronounced features, quirky blue eyes, and open lip sores revealed a story of abuse. She shooed away the sweeper and lowered her voice, "stuff was happening" with Mesa members, she in-formed JJ. Bob's rules—no dope dealing inside the clubhouse—had hurt her business. She had been banished to the "no fun" program.

KC pulled a cigarette from her vest pocket, lit it with the table candle, and said matter-of-factly, "I'm thinking of starting up an escort service. I could use a good business partner. If you're interested, I could put you on the license . . . with Bird's permission of course."

Business partner. Oddly, prostitution leveled the playing field; it gave the women control, power, and income. KC was a survivor in the under-world. In another life she might have been a CEO or a shrewd defense at-torney looking to sell a case. In her limited circle the former runaway and prostitute chose the only paths available to her: drugs and sex.

Undercover operative Bird posing as a Prospect for Hells Angels, Skull Valley, Arizona.

The operatives pose as Solo Angeles Nomads, with a mixture of real outlaws and borrowed federal agents posing as fake bikers. Faces have been blurred to protect identities.

In preparation of the fake Mongol killing, Woody's face and Mongol cuts were smeared with cow's blood (*above and below*). The quality of the photos is grainy because operatives hoped to simulate the crude quality of snapshots they might have taken of the dead body as trophy or "evidence" for the Hells Angels. Woody's face is blurred to protect his identity.

Woody in the ditch as part of the simulated killing of a hated Mongol member.

The FedEx box, draped in an Arizona Hells Angels vest, which contained the "dead" Mongol motorcycle member's vest.

Undercover Bird (*middle*) posing with ATF case agents Joseph Slatalla, a.k.a. "Beef" (*left*) and "Cricket."

Undercover Bird (*left*) with Mesa Hells Angels chapter president Robert Johnston, a.k.a. "Mesa Bob," flanked with another undercover agent (*right*).

Hells Angels infamous Sonny Barger (*center*) posing with undercover agents dressed as Solo Angeles motorcycle club members. Barger boasted that his organization could never be infiltrated by law enforcement.

A Hells Angels Arizona vest with Southwest designation, Filthy Few Patches (signifying that a member has murdered for the club), and Death Head pin.

A Hells Angels Tucson vest with one percent patch and Death Heads.

Bird standing guard outside the Berdoo Charter clubhouse in San Bernardino, CA. with his trusted confidential informant, Pops. This photo was taken by a member of Black Biscuit's surveillance team from inside a van parked several feet away. The faces of Bird and Pops are blurred to protect their identities.

Hells Angels Mesa Club Members Paul Eischeid (*left*) wanted for the murder of Cynthia Garcia, and Calvin Schaeffer, a.k.a. "Cal" (*center*).

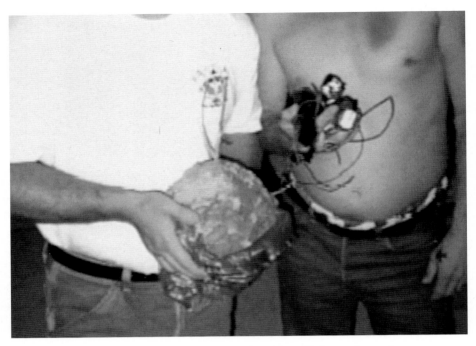
Undercover agents with homemade explosives purchased from Hells Angels members.

Seized weapons cache and old Arizona Dirty Dozen vest after raids.

JJ wasn't being recruited for her business savvy. No, JJ had something KC needed and would never have with the Hells Angels: respect. JJ could funnel clients to KC and take a percentage of the proceeds. The proposition was simple, almost primal. In KC's world the offer made sense as business; after all, it wasn't as if KC could easily leave the biker community without repercussion. She had been branded, as many of the biker women were, with tattoos that boasted, "Property of the Hells Angels."

KC survived the way an animal survives: preying on the weak for sustenance. And whether KC enjoyed the perceived mystique of being a Hells Angel's old lady or simply endured her role as one, she was married to the biker lifestyle and too much an accomplice in the club's criminal exploits to ever leave with its secrets. She reasoned she was safer in their company than alone on the outside forever watching her back.

JJ caught the irony of KC's predicament since she too was prepared to betray KC's trust for the success of Black Biscuit. As close as JJ became with the women, feigning sympathy for their dreadful lives, offering advice to them about the Hells Angels, she never forgot for one moment that these women were Angel guards who would turn on her in a second.

Mesa Bob appeared more agitated than usual by Bird's presence at the clubhouse later that evening having spent the last three days in a methamphetamine-induced stupor. Still high, Bob's gaze darted passed Bird's shoulder to dark corners of the bar, to guests spilling through the door, ever leery of the "shadow people" that lived in the folds of his curtains, watching him.

"I run a tight ship," Mesa Bob reminded Bird, disdainful of "some members" who "ran their lives" by methamphetamine. Control was the key, he emphasized, adding that the damage to Bird's reputation had been "catastrophic." If it were him, Bob sniffed indignantly, he would have "kicked some ass" in Tijuana. Still, Bob assured Bird that he had Bob's endorsement of the Solos at least, but this was conditional—the Solo Angeles nomads needed to consider disbanding and becoming Hells Angels . . . "I would take you, Pops, Timmy, Carlos, Big Al, Sonny, and Steve," Bob tossed in the ATF reinforcements, "but it would have to be done the right way."

* * *

The *right way*, unfortunately, was impractical.

Bird knew what was required to become a full-patched Hells Angel. First, the Solos would have to hang around a chosen charter for a period of weeks or months before committing themselves to further scrutiny and humiliation as official prospects. Not only would the Solos have to assume inferior positions, accepting orders from the Hells Angels like puppets, they would also have to pay a nominal "initiation fee" toward their "background clearance." Essentially, the Solos would be starting over, and, if they chose Mesa to prospect, the likelihood of them being unanimously accepted by all twenty members was risky. They needed a smaller charter, smaller even than Tucson, which had six members.

Beef had threatened to pull the plug before the operatives had another incident. But they were so close, and Bird felt like an actor who, after scoring the lead role in a play, had just been told the show was canceled. But Bird received an unexpected break—"The boys on the river have brokered a deal for you guys to prospect with the soon-to-be-formed Mohave Valley charter," Chef Boy Are Dee informed Bird during a private telephone conversation, "but you might have to start with the Skull Valley charter first."

Days after speaking with Chef Boy Are Dee about Skull Valley, Bird agreed to meet Mesa Bob at the Billet Bar in Scottsdale to discuss what the Mesa Hells Angel chapter president described as the "festering Solo problem." It was late, almost midnight. Bob's tone was tinged with urgency. Something was up. Bird waded through the cluster of Hells Angels gathered amidst smoke and dry ice like strange dark spirits. Hard rock blasted from the jukebox. Tension undercut the clink of beer bottles. He was being set up, betrayed the way he planned to betray Mesa Bob, cold and calculated. *Get out get out get out,* Bird's internal alarms sounded.

But Bird pressed on toward the cube of light where Bob waited for him like a spider, his smile tight and forced, his gaze menacing and accusatory. Heat burned Bird's neck. Bob took a long pull on his beer and advised that his confidant, Guy, had talked trash about the Solo Angeles nomads at the Hells Angels anniversary party. Guy insisted the members were frauds, imposters.

"But I told him you were the real deal," Bob warned, adding, "this isn't good for our public image."

Bird nodded, paused for emphasis, and attempted once more to pacify Bob with his reasons why the Tijuana Solo Angeles had shunned the operatives: The nomads were "white boys" amidst Hispanic brothers; their president, Rudy, had disrespected the Tijuana Solos; they'd worn nomad patches on their vests without Solo permission; but worst of all, the nomads *supported* the Hells Angels.

Bob put up a hand. He had heard enough. He gave Bird an ultimatum: the nomads had "thirty days to fix their problems with the Solos Angeles," or *he* would fix it for them.

Mesa Bob simulated a gun with his hand, put it to Bird's temple, and pulled the trigger.

HEART

Bird started, awake, thoughts of Mesa Bob's earlier threats still fresh in his mind. His eyes adjusted to the murky predawn light in the new under-cover trailer Beef had secured for them after the Chico disaster. The inside resembled a gutted bunkhouse with its few scattered pieces of furniture, frayed rugs, and dirty linoleum. Beef had supplied a few barbells and a weight bench for good measure, but there hadn't been time to indulge in healthy habits and frankly no one really cared. The place felt borrowed, musty, inhabited by the ghosts of victims who had met violent ends. No one complained. Not really. They lived like transients, taking few posses-sions, sleeping on tile or cardboard, eating scraps, living on booze and smoke. Strangely, it had become a way of life for them. Fear kept them alert. Adrenaline kept them alive.

Bird's pager blinked beside him like an angry red eye. Bird glanced at the screen: Beef. Bird had only had an hour of sleep that night and felt half-drugged as he dragged himself off the couch, his legs thick and clumsy in his combat boots. His pulse raced, and he had fleeting thoughts that he might be having a heart attack. Parts of him were numb, sweat soaked the back of his shirt, and sharp pain zipped through his left arm. But such a notion—that he might be sick, *really* sick—was almost silly to Bird. It wasn't as if he could check out for an hour, a day, or even a week and visit the county hospital. He was about to become a Hells Angel prospect and embark on the most important part of the investigation. His life would be scrutinized and his time monitored.

If ATF so much as learned that Bird's health was in jeopardy, brass wouldn't hesitate to shut down the operation, or worse, order his "temporary" removal. Never mind that there was no such thing as respite from undercover life, particularly a *prospect's* life.

Besides, what excuse could he offer that would even make sense? None. Instead, Bird coped with his pain through concentration, transporting his mind to a calmer place, one filled with blue-black ocean swells, gulls, and shells so large he could stick his whole head inside. And he avoided mirrors, unable to register his gray and sickly reflection in the glass. He swallowed Advil hoping to stop the banging in his head.

JJ stirred across from him, curled in a fetal position on the futon by the window. Her Sig Sauer had dropped to the floor. Although she was to be on night watch, JJ had fallen asleep fully clothed. Now, she shot Bird a panicked, apologetic stare, her memories still raw from the Chico threat. She snatched up her gun, scrambled to her feet, her shirt wet with sweat.

Timmy hadn't slept at all. He sat on the kitchen floor, propped against the open refrigerator, cold slabs of raw meat pressed to his forehead. There was no air in the trailer, just swamp coolers that didn't work in rain or humidity. Only Pops seemed strangely reticent, his back to the oven, more afraid of his night demons than anything the Hells Angels proposed.

"Hoover's been assassinated," Beef barked over the line. "A Mongol popped him right outside a Phoenix bar."

Hoover was the Hells Angels former Cave Creek charter president. He had a reputation among outlaw bikers for being a tyrant and was well hated by his peers and enemies. Apparently, Hoover had been executed in the parking lot of Bridgett's Last Laugh, a popular Hells Angels hangout. Rumor had it that Hoover had just mounted his motorcycle with his girlfriend on the back when he slumped over, the victim of a bullet to the back of his head shot at close range. The murder had been swift and silent and committed in the presence of at least fifteen Hells Angels, and yet no one saw the perpetrator and no one was ever apprehended.

Hoover's girlfriend, during a subsequent police interview, confirmed that she had never heard a gunshot. Cops suspected the murderer had used a silencer. Predictably, the Hells Angels informed Hoover's girlfriend that the cops had killed Hoover. And she believed them. The cops, however, had a different notion and suspected the killing had been an inside hit orchestrated by disgruntled Hells Angels who had tired of Hoover's militant leadership. Other unconfirmed rumors blamed Hoover's murder on a Mongol. Bird suspected the Hells Angels had perpetuated the lie to justify their war effort against the outlaw motorcycle group or at least to deflect attention away from the club's illegal activities. Whatever the explanation, it wasn't likely that a Mongol would be foolish enough to execute a Hells Angel president in the presence of his own . . . and live to see another day.

Hoover's death sent a cold ripple through Bird. If the Hells Angels were willing to murder their own in a public, noisy place and escape arrest what would one do to him if provoked?

"It's bullshit," Joby agitated, pacing in the crawl space of an upstairs room in the Cave Creek clubhouse where he had called an emergency meeting with Bird, Timmy, and Pops to discuss the "Hoover situation." Joby's role was to perpetuate the charade that a Mongol had murdered their president, and it was time for retribution. War. Shell, a Cave Creek Hells Angel, sat quietly in a corner of the room, his blue steel semiautomatic pistol resting in his lap. He was more a presence than a participant as he lit a marijuana cigarette thoughtfully and listened to Joby's pitch.

Apparently, Bird was already Hells Angel property—Joby and Bob had begun "negotiating" for Bird's bid. Joby had a strong national influence in the club and was already mildly recruiting another motorcycle gang, the Nazi Low Riders, to become Hells Angels.

"But *you*," Joby gushed, "you need to check us out . . . and bring your old lady," he grinned. "She's a good woman. She'll help you through tough times."

Bird deflected Joby's invitation, temporarily. He had unfinished business with the Solo Angeles in Tijuana. Joby nodded, "I'll wait," and offered his support—two live rounds of 9mm Black Talon ammunition. "Vest busters," in case the cops harassed him.

★ ★ ★

Days later, over bloody steak and potatoes at the Golden Nugget in Wickenburg, Arizona, a small town north of Phoenix, Joby established some ground rules for the operatives. Unofficially, the Solos were now a defunct club, soon to be reborn as prospects under the Hells Angels Skull Valley charter. Joby reminded Bird that he had been Sonny Barger's recruit "four years now"; he proudly counted the time on his fingers. Sonny would be pleased, Joby hinted, if patches were seen in Prescott. In fact Joby hoped the operatives would announce their intentions to the members at church the next week. Joby paused, his fork in midair, meat juice pooling in the center of his plate, "I'll tell you what to say."

Relinquishing control was part of the grooming process. Prospects had no voice. They were mere puppets in a strange road play. It didn't matter what status Bird enjoyed as a Solo, as a Hells Angel recruit he would answer to "prospect," surrender his weapon, and conduct debt collections and drug trafficking for the Hells Angels. He would be a Nobody and so terribly proud.

But smooth transitions were important. Protocol was important. The second act of this "play" had to flow, climax, and end with indictments. They were so close, and yet this last ruse had to be *Masterpiece Theater*. Timmy could barely contain his excitement—"we're in," he gushed, forgetting momentarily the promise of unglamorous and grueling weeks ahead as a Hells Angel prospect. No matter. Timmy was right. They had accomplished the impossible, fooled the Hells Angels, and survived multiple attacks on their credibility. And they had collected enough hard evidence against the club to devastate any future criminal exploits.

And yet, Bird wanted more. They all did. The operation would have felt incomplete had the Solos succumbed to Beef's pleas to surrender before they actually became Hells Angels. But even Beef couldn't resist the temptation to push the envelope, just a little further . . . prospect, get inside Hells Angels operations, and get out before someone really got hurt.

Maybe it *was* ego or a sense of righteous indignation that propelled them—if they didn't fight, who would? The cause was noble and unlike other wars, the objective made sense. Bird imagined combat soldiers must share similar feelings—spurned by urgency, need, and guts, the agents would do what no one else dared because they could, not for selfish notoriety but for the good of their country.

With the promise of reward, Timmy attacked the last days of his Solo Angeles career with gusto, negotiating last-minute deals with Mutt for magazines and methamphetamine. It was business as usual as Mutt huddled with Timmy in the bathroom of the Mesa clubhouse, his customary Colt .45 banging against his hip.

Mutt propped his brown plastic gun case on the urinal and said matter-of-factly to Timmy, "I need to unload this for 800 bucks." It was another Colt .45. Mutt squinted at Timmy, his large jowls nearly quivering under the whir of the ceiling fan. As Timmy inspected the weapon, Mutt offered Timmy "a blast" of methamphetamine. He had a twinkle in his eye, as if to assure Timmy, "You're alright my man . . . you're one of us. This isn't a test." Not like last time.

Timmy bluffed, said he didn't have sufficient funds for the gun and would have to finish the deal another time. But Mutt was relentless, paging Timmy several times throughout the night—"Where've you been?" desperation laced his voice, "when you coming back to get the T-shirts?" Timmy had become expert at the language—"T-shirts," "stuff"—all code names for dope. Even amidst funeral arrangements for Hoover, Mutt's focus was "The Deal."

Trigger met Timmy at the door to the Mesa clubhouse the next morning and escorted him to the billiard room where Mutt paced, his brown plastic case open on the table, the Colt .45 and magazines glowing underneath the white bulb. Mutt looked like he hadn't slept; he was dressed in the same jeans and Polo shirt he had worn the previous afternoon. His Colt .45 swung from his hip, and like a bad film clip, Mutt replayed the scene from the day before, again shoving the plastic baggie at Timmy, "Want a blast?"

White light filtered through the clubhouse now heavily guarded in the wake of Hoover's assassination. Hells Angels swarmed the place wearing firearms openly like accessories. As invincible as Timmy now believed he was, even he backed off. Now was not the time. Out of respect for the dead, Timmy stalled and deflected Mutt. The gun deal could wait.

★ ★ ★

Over 300 Hells Angels gathered at Best's Funeral Services in Phoenix later that day to pay their respects to Hoover. Among the attendees were members from charters across the United States and Europe, all there to pay their respects to Hoover—or at least to *appear* to pay their respects. As Bird stood in the viewing line, he was struck by the perversion of it all—that murderous gangsters actually shed tears, crossed their chests, and cared that one of their own had died. Maybe Bird had it all wrong—it wasn't grief they felt but vengeance. That a Mongol would dare to gun down a Hells Angel in cold blood . . . or one of their own . . . *and get away with it.*

Mesa Bob met Bird at the door with a bear hug, his eyes moist, his breath wispy—"You made it," he said, relieved. The bulge of a handgun pressed into Bird's side, a reminder that the Hells Angels were armed, openly flaunting their arsenal of weapons, though most, if not all, were prohibited possessors. Venue didn't matter. That they were all attending a funeral didn't matter. Technically, they were at war with the Mongols. Women filled the corners of the funeral parlor like dirty pockets ready to conceal weapons and stash dope or other illegal paraphernalia from curious eyes.

JJ dutifully joined them against the wall. Next to tweakers and prostitutes, her appearance was almost too robust, despite the tattoos that snaked her upper arms and wrists. Sex appeal was distracting. Like a siren JJ lured the women into her corner without guilt or remorse. Bird admired JJ for that rare skill—she didn't separate the person from the symbol. Her job was to collect intelligence, to shield Bird from unwanted scrutiny, and to ensure Black Biscuit's mission was accomplished. But it wasn't as if JJ had no feelings. She did. There were moments in the quiet dark of the undercover trailer when she shook uncontrollably, when a small part of her former self crumbled inside, and she looked a mere child too young to be holding a Sig Sauer, to be marking women's lives for prison.

She could accept that ATF viewed her as a badge number, that her identity was erased, and that she could no longer live a "normal" life while embodied in this role. She could accept the anxious stares from women in the grocery aisle, the recoil from young children whose mother's yanked them away from the frightening figure she'd become.

JJ couldn't blame them. Even she now winced at her own reflection in the glass. Once attractive and winsome, JJ barely recognized the face that stared back at her from Bird's motorcycle mirror. That woman had aged too soon. Her eyes were dull as if filmed with layers of dirt. Freckles on her arms were now laced with ink, dark twisted ropes that formed a serpent, a rose, and even a bloody tongue. JJ succumbed to her role and branded herself for authenticity. In the beginning she endured the raw sensation of slapped skin, the burning and itchiness that came with tattooing. But recently there were quiet moments of regret, punctuated by frantic, almost manic efforts to scrub her skin raw, remove the images, and reclaim her past.

What JJ couldn't accept, what none of them could, was sacrifice without reward.

This couldn't all be for nothing.

Days after Hoover's funeral, Bird and the others made plans to travel to Prescott to announce their intention to prospect with the Skull Valley Hells Angels. As their play neared the end of its second act, adrenaline replaced exhaustion. None of them had ever imagined they would be this successful in fooling such a violent criminal enterprise. They had gone deeper than any undercover investigation ever had on the Hells Angels and knew the intimate secrets of its most powerful members.

Even Beef was incredulous, his usually sober expression at times cracking into laughter. "Fucking unbelievable," he repeated often, accepting most, if not all, of the credit for masterminding the theater in the first place. The United States Attorney's Office was more than pleased with the results of the operation, but access into the club's inner workings promised to produce even more evidence of the gang's criminal exploits. Although Bird accepted the praise and awe from his bureaucratic peers and marveled at his team's accomplishments, something sinister nagged at his conscience, something no one else spoke about or acknowledged: things could still go terribly wrong. They could still all be killed. Instinctively, Bird knew they could only go so far before . . . they were all so tired.

Physically, Bird was numb and dizzy from exhaustion more often than he cared to admit. Despite periodic visits home to pay the bills, nod to his wife, and tend to household chores, he hadn't ever been able to rejuvenate. Ironically, he hadn't wanted to worry Barbara. The less she knew, the better. He was protecting her, he justified. *Stupid. Stupid. Stupid.* Nothing he could say would alleviate her fears. It didn't matter how long they had been married. Being a cop's wife was bad enough; being the wife of an undercover cop was something else entirely.

And being the wife of a soon-to-be prospect for the Hells Angels . . . well, that topped even Bird's imagination. While his wife had lived through his other ordeals and identities, Bird knew instinctively that this time would be different. This time there might be no reprieve.

Externally, Bird acquired more tattoos and grizzle on his cheeks; his eyes had dulled to pits and his chiseled features hardened. Over the many months Bird found it increasingly difficult to be a father and husband to his family one hour and an outlaw/criminal the next. And he knew the transitions—slipping in and out of both worlds undetected—would only worsen once he became a prospect. Each visit home shortened as mentally he left his family behind.

Strangely, as Bird stumbled through the rooms of his undercover trailer gathering last items to pack before heading up to Prescott, he found himself suddenly and inexplicably on the floor in the hallway. He was sweating profusely and for a brief moment believed he was dead. As his eyes adjusted to the milky light filtering through the curtains, he felt oddly peaceful. Thoughts of his gorgeous home in Tucson replayed in his head like scenes from a past life. Photo stills in his mind. The sunken garden drew him into a lush desert landscape; a lily pond and frog sounds on a warm summer evening teased him, reminded him of the down time he fantasized about but reserved for a life after . . .

But Bird wasn't sure there would ever really be another way of life for him. Retirement, seclusion, witness protection were all nebulous concepts to him. Shame and guilt warred inside him as he thought of his wife and kids and the life they would be forced to abandon because of him. It didn't matter that he knew that the love of his kids for him was unconditional. He wasn't sure he could forgive himself for their sacrifice.

Something cold pressed against his forehead and voices echoed around him vaguely familiar—"Don't you fucking die on us," JJ blurted close to his ear. Bird's eyes struggled to focus. JJ was on her knees beside him shoving ice-cream sandwiches underneath his shirt in a desperate attempt to bring his soaring temperature down.

Ice cream trickled down his sides, sticky wet and cool. Part of him wanted to laugh at the absurdity of the scene—why they hadn't doused him with ice water from the shower he would never know—the other part of him panicked when he couldn't move.

Bird heard Timmy scramble into the house, trip over a tip of rug that had separated from the nail. He had spent the morning washing his soft tail in preparation for their ride to Prescott and to church where they expected to announce their intentions to prospect. Timmy had rehearsed his personal background the night before, playfully taking on the baritone voices of Joby and Skull Valley charter president, Teddy Toth, aka "Galliano," as he explained to them that he was a martial arts instructor.

JJ was berating Bird, urging him to get to a hospital—"Something's wrong with you," she badgered. "Something's wrong with all of us," Bird wanted to scream, but his throat was clogged. He struggled to sit, to calm his team. He didn't need a hospital. He was fine. He just needed a hundred years of sleep. JJ's face contorted. Her mouth moved, but Bird heard no words. He wasn't going to die. Not now. Not here. Not in this suffocating trailer. Not while he was dressed in a bright orange vest and looked like a crushed Halloween pumpkin.

INSIDE ANGEL

MARCH 2003

Bird recovered enough from his morning ordeal to put on a brave show for his team as they gathered later that evening in the dingy hallway of a Super 8 motel in Prescott to attend their first Skull Valley church meeting. The charter's vice president, Egg Head, an imposing creature with wiry black hair and tough pellet eyes, was one of four members in attendance. The charter's president, Galliano, was out ill. The remaining two officers, Robert Rienstra, aka "Butcher" (the secretary) and Joby (the sergeant at arms) assumed positions by the window blocking any inquisitive eyes from the street.

The operatives had been briefed on church meetings by Pops and Rudy after they attended gatherings of Solo Angeles in Tijuana, but none had ever been invited to attend a Hells Angel meeting until now. Church was a club privilege, reserved for members only. Some of the board was present. The club's secretary, Butcher, a large, heavily tattooed biker who wore a long buck knife on his side, recorded the minutes of the meeting and served as the club's debt collector. He ensured that all membership dues were current and noted whether bikers arrived without their required Harley. Butcher also carried a copy of the Hells Angels bylaws for quick reference and a club roster containing contact information for all Hells Angels members. Joby was the club's sergeant at arms entrusted with club security enforcement and weaponry. He also conducted background checks on new applicants.

Rudy Jaime, aka "Dusty," who was also present, was the wild card. As wide as he was tall, he stood in the corner of the room, arms crossed, eyes narrowed to slits, with a strange wide grin on his face. It looked almost painted on, the kind of expression a collector might find on a spooky foreign doll.

One by one, the operatives recited his carefully crafted credentials. There was no room for improvisation or bullshit, although Bird longed to shout out his true qualifications, his extensive experience as a member of the elite Enhanced Undercover Program (EUP) and as an international instructor of the use of undercover techniques. Since 1987 he had participated in more than 500 operations involving homicides, home invasions, narcotics, and murder-for-hire schemes. And he had infiltrated criminal organizations like the Aryan Brotherhood Prison Gang, the Nevada Volunteers Militia, and the Iron Cross Motorcycle Club. And yet . . . this time, it felt different, larger, and more dangerous.

As each operative surrendered his identity to the officers, Egg Head pressed Bird about the allegiance of the Solos to the "girls"[13]; after all both were Hispanic biker clubs. The feud between the Mongols and Hells Angels originated over the Mongols using *letters* on their vests and jackets that too closely resembled the imprint of the Hells Angels. Such disrespect led to the murder of at least one Mongol member at the Laughlin, Nevada, River Run motorcycle rally in April 2002. In that melee three Hells Angels were also shot to death.

"We're leaving the group *because* the Solo Angeles support the Mongols," Bird fibbed.

"The Solo Angeles no longer exist in Arizona," Egg Head clarified.

"Or in the United States," Joby added, giving Bird a hard stare.

"Finish your business with the Solos," Egg Head ordered. "Next week you'll be hang-arounds."

"Hang-arounds? How many fucking weeks is that going to last?" Bird already heard Timmy's whine in his head.

Although none of the operatives was particularly thrilled with the idea of becoming a "sub-Angel," the lowly position was an important part of the

---

[13] The Hells Angels refer to the Mongols as "girls."

investigation because it provided an unprecedented perspective into the inner chamber of the Hells Angels. In time the operatives would be privy to secretive plots, drug negotiations, and arms deals. As Joby revealed, there was "much to learn about the ways of the Hells Angels"—protocol, "training," and psychology. The Hells Angels were a criminal *organization*, an enterprise of intricate webs, and Bird knew that each level—hang-around, prospect, or full-patched member—would produce valuable biker intelligence.

They couldn't stall any longer. They had no excuse not to pledge their loyalty to the Hells Angels. But first they had to return their Solo vests. Once that was accomplished, Egg Head would provide them with official Skull Valley "hang-around" tabs. The Hells Angels had begun putting a square charter-identifying block on the back of the hang-around's vest, irreverently dubbed by Bird as the "license plate."

The operatives had to learn the rules:

- Shoot Mongols on sight.
- No drug *sales*.

Personal use (of drugs) was fine.

In fact Egg Head and Butcher confided to Bird that they were steroid users partial to "Tes" (testosterone), D-bol (Dianabol), Anavar, and Equipoise (horse steroid).

Dusty smiled broadly and advised that he would happily supply Bird with firearms for his trafficking exploits into Mexico. As if on cue, Bird produced a ruse e-mail he had concocted to himself from a fictitious source—the Mongols had no intention of attending the Laughlin Run motorcycle rally, it read. *In case you were thinking of killing a few more,* Bird added in his mind. Instead, the e-mail informed, the Mongols planned to travel to Mexico at that time of the rally. It didn't matter that Bird had made it all up. If Bird could put off another bloody brawl between the two clubs, he would. Besides, the e-mail served another purpose as well: it revealed to Joby and the other Skull Valley members that Bird was a player, connected and trusted by underground sources.

★ ★ ★

In the days following the operatives' initial church meeting, Bird continued to broker narcotics and firearms transactions with Dusty, score automatic SKS assault rifles, and learn of Dusty's military source for M-16 rifles and rocket-propelled grenades.

"Stay clear of Dusty," Egg Head warned Bird one week later at a bar in El Cajon, California, where the operatives gathered in the rear patio with Joby to receive their official Skull Valley tabs.

"He's dangerous," Egg Head elaborated, referring to Dusty's unsavory associations, excessive drug use, and questionable loyalty to his Hells Angels "brothers."

Dusty was another Cal. Bird appreciated rogues.

In San Diego the operatives received their first official assignment as hang-arounds thanks in part to Timmy's cover story as a martial arts instructor. The Hells Angels considered Timmy's "tough guy" act useful, and it helped that Bird had bashed in a few heads with his baseball bat. Pops . . . well he came with the package, and besides he had already assured Butcher earlier in the week that he was no cop. Cornered like a rat in a wet tunnel, Pops made a difficult but wise choice to ingest methamphetamine. Butcher cut the lines of dope with his knife edge and turned the blade purposefully toward Pops. Had Pops hesitated in the room full of Hells Angels, he would surely have been carved up like tough steak, his head hung on the doorknob as modern art.

"You just passed my test," Butcher grinned as pain shot through Pops's nose. Butcher's "test" came without warning—either it was pure impulse or Butcher had suspected Pops was a snitch and wanted to alleviate his doubts.

The deeper the operatives penetrated the club's core, the more urgent their investigation became. Bird rehearsed Plan B in his mind over and over again—if it happened again, if the Hells Angels suspected they were frauds, if Butcher drew his knife and held it to Bird's throat . . . Even as a mere hang-around, Bird was careful to conceal weakness. Pops had crumbled inside, the strain of living deep cover wore on him like an old shirt, and the Hells Angels began to smell his stink. *Snap out of it,* Bird telegraphed to the old CI, fearful that soon ATF would have to pull him out. But unlike Carlos and Rudy, extricating Pops would likely draw suspicion. Plan B required orchestration—preparation. If Butcher sensed Pops was breaking down, surely others had noticed?

The operatives were given guard duty at the San Diego clubhouse while Angels attended a funeral of one of their own. The job was unglamorous and tedious. Hours ticked by as Bird, Timmy, and Pops stood outside in blistering heat without water or food watching for potential threats. A black Hummer parked in the street. Seated inside was a Hells Angel hang-around with an active felony warrant. "Uncomfortable with the police presence in the area," he had come to the clubhouse to secure his stash of methamphetamine and "iron."[14]

Warm ocean air smacked against Bird's cheeks. The hang-around brushed against him with his black doctor's bag full of firearms. Bird let him pass without protest.

"Some fun, huh?" Timmy grumbled underneath his breath. His face was bright red with perspiration. The wet heat was suffocating.

Bird ignored him. It could have been worse. They could have been given more menial chores like cleaning the clubhouse toilets, sifting through scraps of garbage, licking the soles of members' boots. He had heard horror stories about Hells Angels "training."

Anything was fair game. And this was only the beginning.

---

[14] Firearms.

MR. BIG

As hang-arounds the operatives traveled frequently, attending multiple events, motorcycle runs, and meetings with members of their charter and with other Hells Angels. The objective was to be introduced to as many members as possible. The job of the operatives at this stage was to literally "hang around" the Hells Angels.

"We're fucking waiters," Timmy complained as he hobbled past Bird with his third pitcher of beer in the lobby of the MGM Grand Hotel where the Hells Angels had gathered for their annual fund-raiser poker run in Las Vegas. Alcohol sloshed over the sides of glass and splashed Timmy's shirt. He had spent the last hour making sandwiches with mayonnaise and without, with pickles on the side and pickles in a bun, with ketchup dribbled on fries and ketchup swirled with mustard. Like a gong banging the side of his head, Bird heard the command over and over again coming from inside the hotel bar, "Hang-around, . . ."

Amidst cheers and roars of laughter, Timmy emerged from the drunken pit, his bald head a shiny red sore. For the third time in an hour, Joby had knocked the pitcher from Timmy's hand, scolded his clumsiness in front of other Hells Angels, and ordered Timmy to "fetch him another."

"It is what it is," Bird said, deflecting Timmy's protests.

"How come your shit doesn't stink?" Timmy snapped back.

Bird resisted the urge to punch him. Equity had nothing to do with it, though Bird suspected the Hells Angels had more fun messing with Timmy than trying to fluster Bird. Butcher had ordered Bird to guard the motorcycles and run security checks. Such was the glamorous road to becoming a Hells Angel—it was a tease—you're doing good, you're doing bad, we're your friends, we're your enemies.

"Don't break weak on them," Bird had warned his team before their first church meeting. "Animals can smell fear."

By the time Timmy joined Pops in their hotel room at the Hard Rock, it was seven o'clock in the evening, and as exhausted as Timmy was, he knew his night had barely started. Being a hang-around was, in some ways, worse than being a Solo Angeles. Now there was no down time, no safe haven in which to escape. To make matters worse, they had a roommate: Rod, a Hells Angel nomad hang-around and consummate drug addict.

Pops baited him, said he was out of dope, and watched fascinated as Rod engaged him like a true salesman, lifting his T-shirt to show off his goods. Weed on one side, speed on the other, stashed in small plastic baggies just underneath his waistband. But like a good soldier, Rod obeyed the club rules: No *selling* allowed. Ingestion was fine. Rod even offered to snort the methamphetamine with Pops, no charge.

Timmy glared at Pops. Light shot through a hole in the curtain. Bright neon caught the gold lion's mane outside their window. The last thing Timmy needed tonight was to dodge another test. He watched grim-faced as Rod produced a zipper-style day planner. Tucked inside was his Glock 10mm semiautomatic pistol. With the gun on the table pointed at Timmy, Rod scooped a portion of the methamphetamine from his bag and spread it onto the table. He removed a credit card from his wallet and cut three lines. Timmy stared at the white powder, his mind racing. He watched as Rod rolled a dollar bill and nasally ingested his share. *Think of something,* Timmy panicked. The room was suddenly too small; Timmy's breath was loud in his ear. *You're next, think of something.* Rod clutched his head as if reeling from pain. Timmy seized Rod's almost-overdose as his cue.

"You take the first shower," Timmy insisted, hoping the blast of hot water might thwart a trip to the emergency room. The last thing he needed was a dead man in his bedroom.

"You don't have to tell me twice," Rod said as he bolted to the bathroom and shut the door. Another near miss. With shaking hands, Timmy used the inside plastic wrapper of an empty cigarette box to preserve the drugs until he could transfer the dope into Buddah's custody.

Meanwhile, Bird decided, since they were all gathered in Las Vegas, that it was time to introduce the Hells Angels to Lou, aka "Mr. Big." Lou was a mobster Bird invented to bolster his image as a debt collector for the Las Vegas casinos. The more Bird seduced the Hells Angels into believing he was involved in organized crime, or at the very least had connections with gangsters, the more valuable Bird became to the club. The lure of big business promised to make Bird and his team indispensable to the Hells Angels and expedite their leap from hang-arounds to prospects.

As mere hang-arounds the operatives had limited access to the Hells Angels. At most they were able to eavesdrop on conversations and monitor foot traffic entering and leaving various establishments. Without a strategy the operatives were destined to stay hang-arounds for an indefinite period and effectively stall Black Biscuit's mission.

Bird used the venue of the Las Vegas poker run to embellish his role as a debt collector and to convince the Hells Angels that he was worth more to the club as a bona fide member than he was as a mere hang-around. The Hells Angels had already heard Bird brag about his collection exploits, and they assumed he carried around his baseball bat for enforcement purposes. When they inquired, Bird always shared with them just enough information to keep the Hells Angels satisfied that he knew the debt collection business but not enough to rouse their suspicions. It was a dangerous sales job—any detail awry would sound instant alarms for the Hells Angels.

But Bird was a master wordsmith. "Vegas is like childbirth," Bird insisted one afternoon before the poker run as he sat around a table at his undercover residence with Butcher and Mac, "painful but worth repeating."

JJ busied herself in the kitchen preparing a meal for her guests. Butter sizzled in the frying pan as flanks of steak lay like fresh body parts on the counter. JJ smothered a smile, amused by Bird's banter, as she rubbed black pepper into the meat with one hand and kept her other hand free to pull the trigger of her gun if necessary.

"So how does it work?" Butcher salivated.

"John Doe comes into a casino," Bird bluffed. "The pit bosses and security team identify John as a good risk because he spends money, loses, but most importantly, *covers* his losses. If by chance he wins, the casino staff goes into action. They keep him around. They give him free food, free drinks, free show, and extend him a free night at the hotel. Who would pass up a free ticket to *Nudes on Ice*?

Bird had Butcher's attention.

"The casino keeps him around because John Doe will definitely lose his winnings back to the house. Sometimes the house even fronts John a cash advance. What a great casino," Bird continued.

Butcher's eyes brightened.

"John thinks he's now gambling with the house money. He loses the host's money back to them, plus the rest of his own cash trying to catch up to the front, plus," Bird paused for emphasis, "big plus, the vig. The vigorish. The juice. No Vegas freebies. Big John now has to pay back the front plus the 25 percent interest vig and pay it back now."

Butcher grinned.

"John doesn't have the payback. But that's okay because the casino likes him, and when the pain wears off, he'll be back. He'll get even. He'll pay that front back and take some extra home in the process. Now the Venetian can't very well send their security team over to John's house in Salt Lake City to ask for their money. That would be bad business and bad public relations. What if John tells the security crew to fuck off? Then what? They can't tear John up in his front yard for the neighbors to see while wearing their golf shirts and the Palms logo? Of course not. Who would ever come back to the Palms? Does the Mirage hit crew burn down his house to make their point? No way."

Bird grinned and pointed to his chest, "That's where I come in. The casinos call on a small number of 'hunters' who go get the front back, plus the vig. The hunters are three or four times removed from the big shots. The hunters get the money back and are paid with a percentage of the collection."

In the span of fifteen minutes, Bird had improvised a fantastic story, one he had hinted in bits and pieces of conversation over the course of his exchanges with the club members to lend authenticity to his role. He had convinced the Hells Angels that he was a hunter who knew the collection business inside and out. But to really assume a character, Bird had to complete his persona. He produced business cards and created a cell phone voice message that answered to "Imperial Financial Corporation—specializing in Investment Recovery and Guidance." And Bird ensured that his phone rang constantly—the sign of a wanted man, a busy man, a man with such a reputation that solicitors from all over the country contacted him for hired hits. In truth most of the calls meant nothing—his cover team calling to check in, his daughter calling him from home needing help on her homework.

The theater worked. Bird quietly carried his baseball bat around with him, hoping the Hells Angels would believe he used it to smash people's heads or crush delinquent blackjack players' knees.

"Is it really that easy? The collections?" Butcher pressed.

"My broker calls me and has a collection in San Jose. They have all of the dude's personal information from his Players Club card and his biometrics file. His address, phone number, a picture. I get the information and decide if I want the job. I never settle for less than 10 percent. There are guys who will do it for less, but not me. They know I get the job done. The skills to pay the bills," Bird improvised.

"Guns?" Butcher asked.

"Sometimes. Sometimes not. Always the bat. That sends a message that never needs to be spoken," Bird replied.

"Does it ever get . . . shitty?" Butcher's eyes glinted.

"You guys are the fucking intimidators." Bird was always careful to flatter the members and deflect attention away from the operatives. The trick was never to make the Hells Angels compete for superiority—Bird made sure the club knew that he understood his status as a hang-around in the gang. Still, if Bird could seduce the Hells Angels into wanting to participate in his debt collection business . . .

"Who gets you in, who sets it up?"

"Mr. Big, East Coast Lou. He's my broker." Bird decided the next time the phone rang, no matter who was calling, the Lou charade would continue. As if on cue, Bird's phone rang. The "Mexican Hat Dance" ring.

"Speak of the devil," Bird grinned before he even connected the call.

Beef was on the other line, "You still got the whole crew of assholes in the house?"

"I'm just relaxing with some friends, having a nice meal. JJ's cooking steaks. Excellent as usual. Everything's nice and casual."

JJ glared at Bird, clearly hating this aspect of her role.

"How much longer are those clowns going to stick around?" Beef asked.

"Lou, I can definitely take care of that. If it can wait, I'd like to get on it tomorrow. I'm going to be tied up tonight, but as always, it's your call. You need me now and I'm on a plane. Otherwise I have some all-night house guests," Bird answered.

"As long as everything's good inside, we're good out here. The crew is getting ready to pull a long shift. I'm sending them out on burger runs and piss breaks now. Tell Butcher I said to go fuck himself," Beef added.

"Will do. I'll tell JJ you send your love."

Mac left to use the bathroom and Butcher inched closer to Bird, lowered his voice, his tone sober, "The Hells Angels rule is 'your hustle is your hustle.' No one can break in on you. Your game, you say who plays. If you ever need some help, I'd like to get in, you know, work for you on some collections."

"You have something I want, I have something you want."

"Keep me in mind," Butcher said.

"If I showed up on a collection with a real Hells Angel, . . . that would be cool," Bird said, pleased that his ruse was working.

Timmy and Pops lounged in front of the television oblivious to Bird's exchange. They propped their feet up on the coffee table, boots off, tossing lettuce to the pet iguana in the corner of the room. JJ smirked at them.

"What are you laughing at?" Bird asked.

"Nothing."

"Then stop fucking off and get some more steaks up here," he said, knowing how much she hated being treated like a slave. Bird insisted he treated her that way to impress the Hells Angels.

JJ approached the table, steaks on a plate, and leaned close to Bird's ear as if flirting with him, "There's so much testosterone at this table I'm gonna come up pregnant and there's not a one of you that I'd get with." She gave Bird a peck on the cheek and whispered, "Fuck off."

Bird's steak was burnt black on the bottom.

"How's your steak babe?" JJ smiled.

"Just how I like it. Nice and juicy."

The poker run almost didn't happen. The Hells Angels were having trouble securing rooms for the event. They were competing with another convention. Bird, however, assured them that "Lou" would be able to assist. He dialed his longtime friend, Sergeant Gayland Hammack of the Las Vegas Metropolitan Police Department. Bird had known Gayland since 1996 when Bird and another ATF agent successfully infiltrated the Nevada Volunteers Militia.

"I rarely ask you for a favor," Bird whispered into the phone, mindful that Hells Angels were within earshot. "I'm with the boys. I'm coming to Vegas tonight and I need four rooms."

"It's tight here right now what with the convention . . ." Gayland began.

"I need them for the Angels case."

"Give me ten minutes," Gayland responded.

Bird turned to the Hells Angels, "Lou's checking it out."

Ten minutes later, Bird's phone rang. "I got you four rooms at the Hard Rock, executive suites and no charge. Will that work?"

Bird never questioned how Gayland had pulled it off, but he was grateful to him for the favor. Bird was a hero. He had rescued the annual poker run. But the excitement of securing rooms at the Hard Rock quickly wore off once the Angels arrived at the establishment and were ordered by security to remove their vests.

"I wouldn't take my Hells Angel cut off to take a shit in this place," Butcher spit.

Bird, without saying a word, whipped out his phone and dialed Gayland. "Lou, we're in the parking lot getting jacked by security. They say we can't come in with our cuts on. We ain't taking the patches off."

"Give me a minute," Gayland flustered. It was taboo for a Hells Angel to *wash* his colors never mind remove them. Once initiated a biker wore his colors until they literally fell off his back. The dirtier they looked, the more class the biker gained.

Ten minutes later, as the Hells Angels crew began to mount their motorcycles ready to peel off the property, the security officer returned, contrite and apologetic. "Go right in. Mr. Lou says he apologizes for the mistake. Which one of you is Mr. Bird?"

"Right here."

"Mr. Lou would like to meet with you tonight if your schedule permits."

In the elevator inside the Hard Rock, Butcher ordered Bird, "Call my room in five minutes."

"What's up?" Bird asked.

"Just call my fucking room," Butcher insisted.

As Butcher exited, Bird waited as the elevator doors closed and placed his call. His plan had worked.

"You going to meet Lou tonight?" Butcher's voice rose an octave.

"I don't know, am I?" Bird smothered a grin.

"Set it up, as long as I am going with."

"I'll let you know. Lou is not real big on meeting new people," Bird bluffed and hung up the phone. Minutes later panic surged through Bird. Lou didn't exist.

"Butcher wants to meet Lou," Bird advised Gayland in another phone call. "Can Ray or Al play Lou tonight?" Ray and Al were two old-school Las Vegas detectives who had played the undercover role of an organized crime member better than Al Capone.

"Absolutely, for this, absolutely. The organized crime show right?"

"Usual routine, but tell Ray that these guys are the real thing. This isn't running a game on nobodies. These guys are the Hells Angels."

"We're on for Lou at nine thirty if you're up for it," Bird informed Butcher after the arrangements were made to meet the mobster at the "V" in the Venetian Hotel.

"What should I wear?"

Bird cupped his hand over the phone and laughed to JJ, "He wants to know what to wear."

"Wear whatever you want," Bird answered.

"Lou really wants to meet me?" Butcher sounded like an excited child.

"He wants to see *me*. You're just coming along," Bird clarified. Then to lighten the mood, he added, "He really just wants to see JJ."

The trio, Bird, JJ, and Butcher, headed toward the Venetian Hotel. Rain ran down their faces. Bird's phone rang.

"You with Butcher?" Beef asked.

"Yeah, Lou we're on the way right now. I'm not late, am I?"

"Don't panic," Beef said. "This will work out. Ray is tied up on a last-minute assignment. Go into the bar, same scenario as discussed. Thing is, Lou is going to be played by another guy."

"Are you shitting me?" Bird snapped.

"Gayland says this guy can pull it off. Has he ever let you down?"

"We're almost there." Bird hung up, his anxiety high. JJ sensed something was seriously wrong.

"What's up, Bird?"

"Lou just won a 50K bet on the Jets game," Bird bluffed, feeling sick. The three arrived at the Venetian and Bird led the way. He entered the bar trying to follow Beef's instructions only now he didn't even know who the new Lou was. For the first time since his introduction at the Mesa Hells Angels clubhouse, Bird's confidence waned. How was he supposed to sell Lou as his longtime, well-loved, bragged on boss, when he didn't even know what the gangster *looked* like? *Beef warned you about the street theaters. He told you to tone it down, to knock it off,* Bird reprimanded.

Bird spied a man who looked the part of a mobster. Heavily jeweled with thick gold chains, an earring stud, and a large sapphire ring on his thumb, Lou filled one-half of the booth at the bar. He had a bodyguard standing over his shoulder. *Okay Gayland, so far so good.* Bird approached Lou with Butcher and JJ in tow. Lou stood, grabbed Bird and gave him a kiss on each cheek and a long hug.

"This will work out good, trust me. I know what I'm doing," Lou whispered in Bird's ear.

"Too late now, we're in it. If you're no good, I'm fucked."

Lou gave Bird another hug and reached out to kiss JJ. Bird's anxiety subsided. He spied Beef and Gayland at the bar blending like businessmen discussing a corporate take over.

"You must be Butcher?" Lou said.

"Yeah," Butcher responded immediately puffing out his chest.

"Good. Good. Now sit the fuck down Hells Angel."

Bird's heart skipped a beat as he registered Butcher's stunned expression. Clearly, the Hells Angel wasn't accustomed to being addressed in such irreverent fashion. Butcher sat, but he wasn't happy.

"Now listen to me Butcher, I don't give a fuck about the Hells Angels. Not a single fucking care. You do what you do. My gang is bigger than yours. My gang is badder than yours. My gang is meaner than yours. I can see you coming a mile down the street. You don't know if I'm standing next to you at McDonald's. Anything happens to him," he pointed to Bird, "while he is trying to do this Hells Angels thing, you are going to answer to me. He makes my money for me. He carries my money for me. I trust him to take more money across the country for me than you'll see in ten years. If he wants to be a motorcycle rider, that's his business. But if that shit overlaps with my life, fucks me out of a dollar, if he gets hurt or can't come to work for me when I call, . . . the Hells Angels are going to be disappointed. I'll start burning houses down with the doors locked from the outside. Now give me a minute with Jay."

"With who?" Butcher asked. Bird cringed at Lou's mistake.

"Bird is Jay. Come on. Let me buy you a drink," JJ said, recognizing that Butcher was in need of an ego repair and slightly unnerved at "Lou's" slip-up. Butcher sniffed, followed JJ to the bar, clearly wounded.

"Nice to meet you. How was that?" Lou nodded at Bird.

"A little strong don't you think?"

"I know how a crime boss thinks. A made man doesn't give a white rat's ass about the Hells Angels. We were making money before anyone even invented a motorcycle, let alone started calling themselves Hells Angels. Now bring him back over and let me finish."

Bird shrugged and retrieved Butcher from the bar. Beef and Gayland were sipping cocktails in the background and openly laughing at the play they were witnessing.

"Jay says that you would like to work for me," Lou nodded at Butcher.

"Yes sir," Butcher said, imitating Bird's demeanor with Lou.

"I like you Hells Angel Butcher. You know when to speak and when to shut the fuck up. Paisano. I'll let Jay know when we can use you. Don't fuck up, or you'll lose something."

"Lose something?"

"Good-bye, Butcher. Your dinner and drinks are on me. Enjoy your evening. Jay, I have some weapons coming into town tomorrow if you're interested, I know you like those things, an Uzi pistol, two Mac-10s, a silencer, and a couple of AK-47s. Me, I don't like guns. You can have first shot. I'll call you tomorrow. Good night. JJ, you look beautiful. Take care of my friend, . . . Bird. I guess that's what he's calling himself these days."

Lou waddled off laughing and took his bodyguard with him.

"What did he mean, 'lose something'?" Butcher asked Bird as they waited for the food to arrive.

"Lose something you love, something you want. Your finger, your girl, your dog, you know, . . .something," Bird improvised. "No big deal. It's some kind of Old World Sicilian shit. You won't fuck up. You're a fucking Hells Angel. You're a rock star. Everyone in here is looking at you. Everyone in here wishes they were you." Bird reassured him, watching Butcher inflate. The biker enjoyed feeling important. Their meal arrived, compliments of Lou, and Butcher relaxed. He stabbed his fork into a potato and said, "Lou is just like some of the guys I knew back east. Sopranos guys. You know, Gotti, Bonanno, Mafia hitman shit. Like in the movies." Butcher gushed feeling as if he had passed some kind of test. "You know," he added, trying to impress Bird, "I've kind of lived the life of an organized crime figure . . . involved in extortion, loan sharking, and prostitution, you know racketeering?" Butcher advised that he had participated in so many violent events for the Hells Angels that he would soon replace Joby as the sergeant at arms for the Skull Valley charter. "My enforcement methods draw less attention."

He formed his hand into a mock firearm and pointed his fingers at Bird, "I didn't know how to tell Lou this," he bragged, "but I've done some of this before," Butcher shrugged, "Some call it stupidity, but it takes balls to walk up and shoot someone between the eyes, you know what I mean?" He squinted at Bird waiting for his reaction, and when none came, he returned to his dinner. "It takes a special type of person to kill someone else and be able to live with it," he twitched.

Bird couldn't agree more with Butcher. Special people "took care of business" for the Hells Angels.

"Anomity," Butcher tapped his chest as he bragged about business he had "taken care of" for his prison brothers, favors they would never know about. "Anomity" Butcher repeated unaware that he had mispronounced the word *anonymous* twice.

Butcher added that he became a Hells Angel in record time because he handled business, implying that Bird too could ride the fast track to membership by "taking care of business." "Three can keep a secret if two are dead," Butcher whispered, chewing thoughtfully on a piece of steak. A slow grin spread across his face. "Sometimes I wait four or five years for payback." Butcher swallowed and sobered, "I'm the guy who will be standing next to your pillow at 3:00 A.M."

After dinner Bird dropped Butcher off at the Hard Rock and dialed Gayland for his report card.

"How did I do?"

"Lou said he played it like a real family boss would have."

"I don't know where you found him last minute, but he was good. Butcher bought it," Bird said.

"He better be good. He's a crime boss from New Jersey who came out here and fucked up. We caught him and turned him over for us. He's our new organized crime snitch-informant. He wasn't faking it. He was the real deal."

Bird hung up the phone and smiled. Gayland had never let him down.

The next day at the First Annual Strip Poker Run, Butcher pestered Bird about Lou's delivery—"Have you heard anything?" Butcher was hyper, seemingly thrilled by the prospect of being part of organized crime. He phoned Bird four times in the course of an hour, his question a bad echo over the line. Bird let Butcher sweat it out until six o'clock that afternoon in part because he had to recruit Buddha to complete the ruse.

"From who?" Bird teased.

"Lou, about the guns."

Butcher was especially harsh on Bird after having been humiliated by Lou the previous evening. He had Bird running for beers, burgers, cigarettes—reestablishing the hierarchy just in case Bird needed reminders. Bird's phone rang.

"We'll meet you at the Club Palomino. Send them here and JJ, bring my cash bag," Bird instructed as he cradled the phone between his ear and shoulder pretending to make arrangements with his fictitious mobster to collect the shipment of guns.

"Lou?" Butcher asked anxiously over the other line.

"Yeah, he's sending someone over with the hardware," Bird explained.

Later in the Palomino parking lot, JJ arrived with Buddah driving the war wagon, the government-issued undercover car, pulling the motorcycle trailer. A cluster of Hells Angels gathered in the parking lot to watch the exchange. They straddled car hoods, leaned against wire fencing and huddled in doorways.

"Look at this fucker," Bird teased Buddah who was playing Lou's gun trafficker. "They sent a Samoan. Butcher watch my back." Butcher, who had tagged along as Bird's bodyguard, blanched at Bird's command, not at all pleased at the role reversal or the humiliation in front of other Hells Angels. Bird took orders from *Butcher* and not the other way around. Still, Butcher, unsure what else to do, dutifully followed Bird's lead.

Please Buddha, stay cool, this jackass will shoot you in front of his brothers for any number of reasons. Bird knew Butcher wanted to do a good job on his first report card back to Lou. He needed to get an "A."

Bird greeted Buddha as if he had never met him before. Buddha and JJ led Bird to the trailer, which was locked with padlocks. Bird climbed inside and examined the weapons. *Un-fucking-believable,* Bird cursed under his breath. No one had bothered to remove the safety ties from the firearms when they removed them from the vault.

"What's with the ties?" Butcher asked.

Bird, laughing at the situation, and thinking quickly said, "Fucking Lou, he's scared shitless of guns." He continued to examine the weapons, field testing the machine guns for fully automatic function.

"When you got the juice like Lou, other people carry your guns for you," Buddha said stiffly, not a whiz at acting.

Bird sensed Butcher was uncomfortable. Whether Butcher was anxious because he was negotiating a gun deal in a parking lot in the middle of Las Vegas with scores of police and Hells Angels around or because Bird had slipped was difficult to tell.

"All or nothing Bird," Buddha said. "Five G's or they're going to LA, so make up your mind. All these bikers here are freaking me out." He was trying to speed things along.

"Five grand it is," Bird said. "JJ pay him and get these out of here." JJ and Buddha left in the truck with the guns. Bird slipped a one hundred dollar bill to Butcher.

"That's how easy it is—five minutes, a hundred dollars," Bird said.

"If it was up to Butcher," his wife, Stacey, matter-of-factly confided to JJ over dinner later that night, "he would put a full patch on Bird right now, but he has to follow certain procedures." She took a long pull on her Heineken and said thoughtfully, "I wouldn't be surprised if he puts a bottom rocker on Bird at the next Skull Valley meeting.

"Bird's moving fast through the process. I've never seen Butcher take to anyone the way he has with Bird . . . except of course to Galliano," Stacey added. She slid her beer to the side and squeezed JJ's hand. "You're practically family," Stacey gushed. She reached into her purse and offered Bird a Xanax pill. Bird frowned and politely declined. "Not while I'm protecting Butcher," he qualified. As a hang-around security guard, he had been ordered to refrain from drugs and alcohol. He needed to "keep a clear head" in case of trouble.

It was after midnight when Bird escorted Butcher and Stacey to their hotel room. While on the elevator Stacey again offered Bird the Xanax tablets, pouring the pills into her hand from a prescription bottle. She pressed the light blue tablets into Bird's hands. Butcher hovered over him exposing his Bersa .380 caliber pistol.

"They'll help you sleep," Stacey smiled and added, "but you didn't get them from me."

"We're going to turn you into a pill popper," Butcher laughed and slapped Bird on the back.

Bird watched as the two slipped into the hotel room like dark spirits and turned to leave. It had been a long night and he felt oddly disconnected as he walked the bright streets surrounding the Hard Rock Hotel. It was almost pointless to sleep. He half considered ducking into a nearby coffee shop just to inhale the smell of grits and coffee, just to feel *normal*, just to feel anything but numb.

PROTOCOL

At Butcher's request Stacey rode with JJ in the undercover van back to Arizona. Stacey claimed to have once broken her back and couldn't withstand the pounding of Butcher's motorcycle. JJ suspected the story was a ruse that Stacey used to fool law enforcement when she smuggled or concealed deliveries for Butcher.

Apparently, Stacey had once attended nursing school but was expelled because she was a felon. More precisely, Stacey was a "career criminal" who should have been serving fifteen years to life in Texas but for a bureaucratic error that had mistakenly voided all her charges.

She was a waif, a mere slither of a woman, with sunken eyes, a flat chest, and a mop of oily blond hair. Stacey was disarming, too weak looking to raise the suspicion of law enforcement or pose a credible threat and yet . . . she was spry and sharp enough to play the system. She had paperwork—whether real or manufactured—detailing her back injury, documents she carried with her and used to her advantage.

"No guns in here, officer," she mocked as Bird warned them about the Hoover Dam inspection point. With a broken back—real or imagined— no officer would dare ask her to move.

Stacey winked at JJ and pointed to her purse. "Betty Sue's inside," she smiled. "And I got more 'bang bangs' stashed underneath my seat." Her ruse was simply to lie on the guns, wave her medical papers at the cops, and avoid having to move. "Broken back officers," she snapped her bubble gum. What could the cops say to that?

Just outside Kingman, Arizona, Butcher's motorcycle broke down. His tire shred. Rather than risk the Department of Public Safety's (DPS) contact, Butcher loaded his bike into the undercover trailer. Butcher was almost apologetic as Bird scurried around assisting him with the motorcycle parts. He put a hand to his chest and explained, "The reason why the Hells Angels prospecting period is longer than most clubs is because it prevents infiltration into the Hells Angels by law enforcement. We don't want to make it too easy for them," Butcher winked, no doubt alluding to the "easy" infiltration of the Sons of Silence Motorcycle Club by Colorado law enforcement.

"The cops don't have patience to get through our protocol," Butcher said dismissively. "We're going to groom you guys," he added. "You should become members fast," Butcher snapped his fingers.

That may have been true, but Timmy had had enough. He had tired of being the biker's whipping post. One week after the poker run, he telephoned Egg Head and asked him to sponsor him into the Hells Angels.

"What's the matter with you?" Bird scowled.

"Doesn't hurt to ask," Timmy countered.

"There's a process dumb shit," Bird scolded.

"And I'm speeding it up."

Incredibly, Egg Head accepted the responsibility and asked Timmy to meet with him. He was interested in selling firearms to Timmy. "Do you care if they're stolen?" he inquired, explaining that he had recently sold two Tec-9 firearms and an M-1.

Egg Head didn't wait for Timmy's reply. Instead he launched into a monologue about the "Hells Angel" way of doing business. It was about revenge. When Egg Head felt compromised, he simply took collateral—tools, vehicles, an air compressor, industrial vacuum, a pressure washer, whatever was "available"—and he felt vindicated. But sometimes property wasn't enough.

Sometimes assaults were necessary. Even murder.

The Skull Valley clubhouse, located in Chino Valley, was heavily guarded, with two pit bulls and a hybrid wolf chained to a barbed wire fence surrounding the property. Two German shepherds guarded the inside of the clubhouse, their cages strategically placed at various entrances and exits. The clubhouse was meant to be a safe haven, a place where members discussed Angels business, confessed to criminal activity, and sought refuge when the shit broke. Inside, there was a designated war room where the bikers stashed an arsenal of weapons in case of armed confrontation.

Although hang-arounds were typically prohibited from participating in church, Joby ushered the operatives into a side room before the official meeting began, patted them down for wires and recording devices, and drilled them about their possible law enforcement contact. It didn't matter that they had pledged their allegiance to the Hells Angels, trust was a risk none of the bikers could afford to take. There were mutinies brewing even among full-patched brothers who mistrusted or disapproved of each other's reckless habits—Cal, Mac, who, because of his probationary status, had been placed on a nonassociation status, and Butcher, who vied for Joby's title.

Galliano, the club's elderly president, nodded approvingly from his armchair, his oxygen tank close by. The shakedown was meant to remind the operatives who was boss and to warn them not to become too complacent. The club had high expectations of them: killing a Mongol would make the members proud.

Egg Head cornered Timmy afterward. He had heard about the exchange with Lou in Las Vegas, and he wanted to be included in the debt collections. "He'll want to meet you," Timmy cautioned. "Lou doesn't do business with strangers."

Egg Head glanced over his shoulder to make sure the others weren't listening and said, "Galliano won't approve. He used to do a lot of that stuff for the New York Mafia. He doesn't think it's worth risking his life in prison. Still," he paused, rubbed his lower chin and said thoughtfully, "sometimes I'm into that shit and sometimes I'm not. I used to deal cocaine with the Italian Mafia," he bragged, and added, "I've tied up victims with duct tape." Then, Egg Head waited a beat and said softly, "I could use the extra cash. Besides, I'm due for a tune-up."

Timmy understood "tune-up" to mean "assault."

"You can't wear your colors," Timmy warned him.

"Not a problem," Egg Head shrugged. He had covered up his tattoos before.

"I'll make the arrangements." Timmy assured him.

"Get me my gun," Galliano ordered Bird finally. The 9mm pistol was secured in a black nylon holster in Galliano's truck. Bird scurried to the vehicle, retrieved the firearm, and dutifully delivered it to the president. Galliano nodded approvingly as if he were training a pet dog and had just tossed it a bone. He ordered Joby to leave the room.

"Don't trust Joby or Dusty," Galliano said in a lowered voice, "and don't use the word *outlaw*," he admonished Pops. "We live on the dark side."

Bird then produced $500 in cash as his donation to the Skull Valley charter, "compliments of Lou." Galliano visibly tensed at the offering. "You're under no obligation to give us the profits from your firearms trafficking business," he wheezed. "Prospective members cannot buy their way into the Hells Angels."

"I wouldn't want the position if that was so," Bird replied coolly.

"Don't be too eager to become a member," Galliano cautioned. "Your enthusiasm could be misinterpreted." He tapped his chest, "I live, eat, sleep, breathe, and shit the Hells Angels. It is my life."

Galliano squinted at Bird, motioned to Bird's hand, and frowned. Bird wore an "SS" lightning bolt ring on his finger. Galliano advised that the Hells Angels in the United States had agreed to outlaw the use of the "SS" symbol on all paraphernalia out of deference to their German brothers. The fine for wearing one was $500.

Bird removed his ring.

FALSE ALARM

MAY 2003

Later, in the predawn hours, with rain pelting down outside, Bird was startled awake from a shallow, restless sleep, by pounding on his trailer door. Now what? The whole team stirred, their movements synchronized as each slipped on his boots, loaded a clip into a nearby gun, and assumed a defensive position. JJ crawled beneath the couch, lying on her belly, her Sig Sauer pointed at the door. Pops pressed against the kitchen wall, his hands chest level as his finger grazed the trigger. Timmy made eye contact with Bird, ducked into the bathroom, and shut the pocket door. A pall of apprehension filled the air. Bird could hear the pounding of his own heart as he moved toward the door, and using his gun barrel, he bent a slat of vinyl blind on the living room window and peered outside. Beneath the bald porch light, Butcher stood, water streaming down his face.

A chill pricked Bird's neck. It was four o'clock in the morning. What the hell was Butcher doing on his doorstep, with one hand tucked suspiciously inside his vest as if protecting his gun from the rain? More importantly, how long had the Hells Angel been out there? And if Butcher hadn't announced his presence . . .? Bird released the slat, motioned for the others to keep quiet, and with a deep breath, cracked open the trailer door. A blast of cool wind smacked his face.

Butcher grinned, seemingly unfazed by the downpour.

"Just checking up on you guys," He said, peering over Bird's shoulder into the dark trailer.

Bird knew better than to ask for clarification although he wondered if Butcher's impromptu visit counted as part of his special "enforcement methods." He had traveled alone, parking his Harley in the gravel. Hard to tell whether Butcher's presence was meant to intimidate, harass, or warn the operatives that they were still lowly hang-arounds and technically Hells Angel property. Galliano's advice resounded in his head—Bird had to learn about the ways of the Hells Angels and observe proper protocol. Guys who fucked up got a bat to their head.

Bird swallowed, searching for a calm response, "You're early," he managed. "I'm not scheduled to sell T-shirts at the run until two thirty this afternoon." He was fairly certain Butcher hadn't paid him a visit to confirm his sales schedule at the vendor's booth.

Butcher chuckled, removed his hand from inside his vest, and tucked his gun into his waistband. "I like humor." He glanced back at the empty street as if expecting reinforcements.

Bird's heart raced, steady, steady . . . no sudden movements or he might send the other operatives the wrong signal. Where the hell was his surveillance crew? His fingers tightened around his gun.

"Don't be late," Butcher winked and walked backward toward his motorcycle. Rain splashed off his moustache and slick bald head. "You look a little stressed," he added. "Come by after the run. My wife will fix you up."

But Bird avoided an afternoon of pill-popping Somas. After a full day of selling T-shirts at the motorcycle run, Joby ordered him to house-sit his residence while he and his girlfriend left town for the night. Thankfully, the assignment required him to be alert and drug-free, an excuse Butcher readily accepted. It was after nine that night when Bird and JJ arrived at Joby's place, reviewed detailed instructions on how to enter the house, and found the keys to Joby's gun chest on the kitchen table "in case they wanted to shoot any."

From an investigative stance Joby's invitation provided invaluable intelligence—a voyeuristic view into an Angel's lifestyle. Not only did Bird need a map to access the entrance to the house, but also once inside, the place was a vault of paraphernalia, from a marijuana garden to an arsenal of illegal weapons—Mac-11, .12 gauge and .20 gauge shotguns, Commando Mark V .45 caliber rifles. The walls were littered with headshots of Hells Angels, including photos of the Solos Angeles posing with key club members. The pictures formed an eerie documentary of their infiltration.

As was typical of the Hells Angel lifestyle, Bird had a night visitor: Silent Steve. The biker was obsessed over the shooting death of his son one year earlier and had a proposition for Bird. He needed a hit man. He met with Bird in the kitchen of Joby's house after midnight. Half of the bulbs had burned out, the other half flickered above them as if a reminder that time was short and soon they would both be sitting in darkness.

Silent Steve wore the death of his son like an old skin he couldn't shed. He made a strange image—his large muscular frame straddling nearly two stools at the table revealed a dangerous vulnerability. Bird decided it wasn't sorrow that fueled the biker's rage: it was his need for revenge. He hadn't come here tonight to reminisce about his dead son; he had come to plot a murder. Bird thought about his own son and felt his chest constrict. No parent should ever survive the death of his child. Not even a Hells Angel.

Bird felt a wedge of guilt in his throat. Silent Steve had sought him out in desperation, in confidence, and in raw, palpable grief. Bird wasn't certain what disturbed him more—that he could relate to the biker as a father and as a human being with a conscience or that he planned to betray him and send him to prison?

Silent Steve produced the chest X-ray of the .25 caliber bullet lodged in his son's ribs. As he retold the sordid tale of sloppy police investigation, the veins in his neck bulged like wet ropes. Despite multiple eyewitnesses and a confession from the shooter, no one had been arrested.

Silent Steve suspected the Mexican Mafia.

Bird listened intently as the biker described in gruesome detail how he hoped to kidnap the killer and torture him with a butane torch. "I'd have dismembered the son of a bitch myself except that the cops would immediately have accused me," he said matter-of-factly.

"The murder has to look like something other than retaliation," Bird agreed, giving a brilliant performance as a hit man. "Let me work the suspect.

You're too well known in these parts," he added, hoping to deflect Silent Steve's venom and curb his vigilantism.

The biker mulled over Bird's suggestion and shrugged, "If I'm wrong about this guy, I'd feel bad about it, but I'd get over it."

JJ wasn't privy to Silent Steve's murder plot. She was on her own intelligence-gathering mission, having agreed to meet Butcher's wife, Stacey, at the Pinion Pines Bar and "learn the ways of the Hells Angels" from the female perspective. The place was noisy, full of a mixed biker crowd. Several dancers made love to poles on center stage.

Stacey waved JJ over to a dark corner booth where she was joined by Galliano's stripper girlfriend. The dancer used a stage name although JJ couldn't imagine what identity the young working girl hoped to conceal. Her life was troubled, rife with violence and abuse. She ran with a fast, wild crowd. Although she was young enough to be Galliano's daughter, her face told another story: hard-edged and deeply creased like stone carved by the rain. She had lived on the streets since she was eleven and had probably ingested drugs and pills for as many years.

In addition to using methamphetamine, most of the women JJ encountered were pill-poppers—Xanax, Ecstasy, Somas. In the dim lights of the bar, Stacey explained to JJ yet again how to be a good old lady, rules JJ needed to learn if she was to be Bird's girl: (1) Do not talk to other men. (2) Do not sit at the bar—sit at the back of the bar and do not bring attention to yourself. (3) Do not discuss Hells Angels business with anyone. (4) When the guys are talking about business, walk away.

Stacey spoke slowly as if talking underwater and yet her face brightened at the prospect of "training" JJ. Stacey was finally, painfully, important. She held the secrets to proper protocol, and she relished her mentoring role. In a world that belittled women, relegated them to wallpaper, Stacey suddenly had purpose. Like a mother hen she doled out tablets to the dancers as if the pills were a gift, a magical transport to a world Outside.

"Take one," Stacey offered JJ a Xanax.

"Thanks," JJ said slipping the pill into her pocket.

"No," Stacey shook her head in earnest. "You need to take the pill now.

I've never seen you take one yet," she said suddenly dejected, cupping JJ's face in her hands and forcing a blue pill into JJ's mouth. Stacey watched her intently, a flicker of doubt lingering in her black eyes, flint chips that glinted like quartz crystals.

"Put it on your tongue," Stacy instructed.

JJ nodded, and a few seconds later, when Stacey turned her head, JJ spit the pill into her beer bottle.

ALMOST ANGELS

MAY 2003

The operatives selected the Skull Valley charter to hang around because the members sanctioned their continued arms and drug trafficking, and by so doing they allowed the operatives to build a compelling case against the Hells Angels. The operation was now in its sixteenth month and nerves were shot.

There had been unconfirmed rumors that splinter groups within the Hells Angels were grumbling about the popularity of the former Solos, their seemingly lightening speed through protocol, their mysterious and sudden appearance in Mesa as nomad Solo Angeles. Despite the frequent trips the operatives made to Tijuana to legitimize their presence and back stories, there were still renegades in the Hells Angels who wanted nothing more than to see them disappear, or more accurately, to see *Bird* disappear. Some believed Bird threatened the power structure of the Angels by his bold outspoken confidence. Beef worried that these outlaws might begin researching Bird's background.

Again, Beef warned the team that trouble might be brewing, that maybe it was time to shut down the operation. They had accomplished more than they had ever imagined. They had infiltrated the club and gathered enough intelligence on the bikers to feed even the hungriest prosecutors. And yet, there was a lingering sense that something was missing, a sense that if the operatives had gotten this far, how much further could they get? The mission, Beef reminded Bird almost daily during heated discussions on the subject, was never to become Hells Angels. Being a prospect was merely a fringe benefit, not a prerequisite to the operation's mission. Beef fretted about liability, risk, and justification to ATF suits, especially as the operation progressed to new heights of danger.

There was an unsettling calm in the air, a strange stillness that was almost surreal, as if noxious fumes had been released into the atmosphere, but the poison had not yet claimed its victims.

Bird set an exhausting pace—arranging meth deals with hang-around Rod in his home in Kingman, Arizona. Rod's residence resembled a bunker, fortified with a Glock, a Norinco, a Mac-90 pistol, an AR-15 rifle with scope, and a .12 gauge shotgun. Soon he hoped to add silencers to his collection.

It was just after dawn when Bird followed Rod into his home office and watched as his girlfriend arrived in an old Honda transporting the drugs. She was a gaunt, pale thing who resembled more ostrich than woman, with thin hair shaved close to her scalp like blond fuzz. She walked bowlegged into the kitchen as if she had a pole shoved up her rear. Soaked with sweat, she managed a tight smile though she was missing a front tooth.

"I was scared while coming here," she confessed, laughing nervously. "So I put the meth in my pants." All six ounces of high-quality glass, the size of an adult male fist. Not an especially attractive image.

"First time jitters," Rod shrugged apologetically as he tucked his Glock inside his waistband and split the drugs with Bird.

The Skull Valley charter had instigated a terror campaign in the city of Prescott to rid the area of other motorcycle gangs. Butcher aimed to dominate the territory, harass other clubs who muscled their way in, and recruit hostile gang members to "flip" and join the Hells Angels. Bird became Butcher's scout, hanging out at local Harley shops, searching for likely targets. Timmy, meanwhile, was ordered to plan assaults for Egg Head and then unplan them at his whim. It was all part of the Hells Angels campaign to intimidate. Timmy had learned not to complain or to ask too many questions. He just *did*. Sometimes in the span of hours, Timmy was ordered to appear at functions in Prescott only to travel to Mesa to meet prospects there. The objective was always the same—to meet and greet prospects and seduce them to join the Skull Valley charter.

After days of complying with members' orders, Butcher left a phone message for Timmy; a package was waiting for him at the Cave Creek clubhouse: *Spa Bob has it. Meet him at 8:00 P.M.*

"I don't like it." Beef was suspicious. He paced the warehouse at headquarters, his nerves frazzled.

"I doubt it's a bomb," Timmy said. He had a point. If the Hells Angels wanted to kill him, any of them, they wouldn't do it with an explosive. They were into guns, silencers, pills.

"Bring it back here to be X-rayed," Beef instructed.

At 8:00 P.M. sharp Timmy met Spa Bob in the parking lot of the Cave Creek clubhouse. The Hells Angel was compact, his arms thick as trees, a large snake tattoo slithered down the bridge of his nose. Without a word of explanation, the biker handed Timmy a brown package and ordered him to deliver it to Butcher the next day. Timmy felt the hair on the back of his neck prick. Why would they need a middleman unless they were testing Timmy? *Would he deliver the package as ordered? Would he turn it over to his fed buddies? Or, would he sample the goods himself?* Timmy imagined what the Angels might be thinking. Timmy stared at the package, neatly sealed with grey packing tape. There was no lettering. No address. No label on the outside at all. Timmy held the package close to his ear. No ticking.

"What the hell is it do you think?" Timmy asked anxiously as he delivered the package to headquarters to be X-rayed. Bird shrugged, his mind reviewing the last few days. Had they made any errors? Had he said something, done something, looked at someone wrong? The package made no sense. The operatives were making progress, mixing well with members, securing drug and arms deals with key players. Where had they fouled up?

"It's a fucking cloth," Beef exclaimed, staring over the radiologist's shoulders at the X-ray.

"Not just cloth," Bird clarified, studying the arches in the image and feeling his pulse race. "Patches. They want to promote us, to make us official Hells Angel *prospects*."

"Low-ranking snouts," Buddha roared from the background. He was watching a Discovery channel program about African tundra wildlife. The show described the animal hierarchy—a wildlife class system Bird and the others immediately saw as analogous to their situation. The elephants, lions, tigers, gazelles were all members and each served a dignified purpose. At the bottom of the food chain were the wild dogs—the hangarounds. The desert dogs were "the cleaners" responsible for licking the blood and skin from decaying carcasses after the predators had picked the bones raw. "The dingos feed and survive only after the larger and more vicious animals give them room," the narrator droned. "They are the lowest ranking of all the snouts."

The moniker fit; Bird had a mind to ask the Hells Angels if he could have a vest tab embroidered with the name, "Low-Ranking Snouts."

Maybe it was too late. The snouts had already apparently advanced to the next level: prospects. They were about to receive their bottom rockers signifying that they were "Arizona" Skull Valley prospects.

At eleven the next morning, Timmy delivered the brown package to Butcher at the Skull Valley clubhouse as ordered. Pops and Bird accompanied him, prepared to guard the premises during the regularly scheduled church meeting. But Galliano had other plans.

As the sickly biker wheeled his oxygen tank closer to the members, he nodded to Joby, giving him permission to speak. Butcher ushered the operatives into the meeting room and shut the door. Joby paced the room, his deliberate strides smacking of urgency. In an unprecedented move, Joby brokered a firearms deal with the operatives. The plan was for the operatives to deliver over twenty handguns to a Hells Angel member in San Francisco who would then sell the weapons to friendly street gangs and split the profits with the operatives.

Although the operatives were technically lowly "hang-arounds," the officers clearly considered them viable members without the official patch. Galliano snapped his fingers at Bird and ordered him to collect several Hells Angels members in Prescott and deliver them to the Skull Valley clubhouse for church. Then, for over an hour Bird, Timmy, and Pops guarded the meeting. They heard shouts from inside, profanity, even a thud against the door. And then Joby slid back the dead bolt and hollered at Timmy, "Get the trailer. Help Egg Head load up his motorcycle."

Timmy knew better than to ask questions. Dusty watched from the sidelines, his inane grin unnerving Timmy. After Timmy loaded up Egg Head's bike, Dusty snapped his fingers and ordered Timmy into the car with him. They were going for a drive to Dusty's tattoo shop.

"He's expired man," Dusty explained, his speech nearly unintelligible through his thick Mexican accent.

"Expired?"

"Out of the club man," Dusty grinned. "You're coming along in case he gets out of hand."

"What should I do?" Timmy played dumb.

"Fuck him up," Dusty said.

"Do you expect him to resist?"

Dusty shrugged. Did it matter?

Timmy would never know exactly what had precipitated Egg Head's demise. As a hang-around Timmy was given sound bites, ordered to co-operate, and praised for his discretion. He would never know why Egg Head was tossed.

Dusty wagged his head and grinned. He was a man of few words. Half full. He maneuvered the trailer into the parking lot of his tattoo shop, shut off the engine, and opened the door. Timmy followed him inside and stood in the shadows. *Just in case.* Egg Head lumbered into the darkness, betrayal in his eyes. Dusty shoved him into a chair, fixed a 9mm Glock to his head, and fired up his tattoo needle. With careful precision he tattooed "out 05–31–03" in three locations on Egg Head's body.

And as a final degradation, Dusty inked out the biker's coveted Death Head tattoo. When a Hells Angel leaves the club under bad terms, the Death Head is obliterated and all the biker's possessions confiscated.

After Egg Head's excommunication from the Hells Angels, the opera-tives returned to the clubhouse; they were asked to join the remaining members. In an unceremonious display of appreciation, Galliano tossed each one of them prospect rockers. "Fast trackers," the president smiled approvingly. "You guys will make it quick. You should introduce yourself like this. 'Bird, prospect for Skull Valley.' Nothing more. Nothing less. No one gives a shit about you guys anyway."

Bird's heart raced as he traced the coveted piece of cloth in his hands, his "colors." All he needed now was that center patch . . . just one more patch and he would *be* a Hells Angel. He caught himself, sneaked a glance at Timmy, whose face had burst into sweat. Relief mixed with pride. They had waited so many months for this symbol of acceptance. They should have been dead many times over and yet . . . there they stood, three ordinary men who had just accomplished something extraordinary.

Bird wanted to whoop like a fan at a football game, release all his tension in a good long cry, hug his cast and crew until their ribs ached, but instead he swallowed the lump in his throat, blinked back the burn in his eyes, and quietly smiled. They had "made it." They were now prospects—and practically home.

RUSSIAN ROULETTE

MAY 2003

Just days after becoming official prospects, Joby announced matter-of-factly over tacos and refried beans at a local Mexican restaurant that the operatives should prepare to die later that evening for the Hells Angels. The Las Vegas charter anticipated a shootout to occur involving the Banditos Motorcycle Club during the Angels scheduled Nevada coalition meeting.

"You should anticipate an armed confrontation," Joby crunched into his beef taco. "And you'll probably go to jail or have to leave the country afterwards if you're still alive."

"Don't bring any items or clothing associated with the Hells Angels," Butcher added, scraping his refried beans to the side of his plate. "We're going undercover."

"I plan to bring my shotgun," Joby declared. "But I'm not going to be 'front line' like I was for the Laughlin shootout."

Joby referred to the year before when Hells Angels members entered the Harrah's Casino in Laughlin to support members from the San Francisco charter and to kill Mongols. Now the Skull Valley charter had pledged their support to the Las Vegas charter for selfish reasons: they were protecting their territory. If the Banditos were successful they would likely infiltrate Arizona. "If they so much as dismount their motorcycles, kill them," Joby ordered.

KERRIE DROBAN

Apparently, Galliano had "struggled" over whom to send to the confrontation; his best or his disposable "soldiers." He couldn't very well send all of the members. The prospect of rebuilding the Skull Valley charter after everyone had died was too daunting. Instead, Galliano sacrificed the operatives and commissioned Joby to be their guide.

"Follow my lead," Joby encouraged, although like a good general, he made it clear to the operatives that if things got heated, he wasn't going to risk his own skin.

Bird wasn't sure whether to feel flattered or sick. Timmy's leg started to twitch uncontrollably under the table, and Pops blanched as he stared at his plate of shredded pork. Of course they were going. There was no question the operatives were headed to Las Vegas. They were prospects and groomed to obey orders. If they didn't do what they were expected to do, they would be killed. This couldn't be it, Bird tensed. They hadn't worked this hard for it all to end now. Pops promptly vomited into his plate.

Joby laughed, "It's okay, Pops. All you've got to do is pull the trigger."

As a parting gift Galliano supplied Joby with an altered "customized" sawed-off shotgun, which Joby loaded into the Jeep Cherokee along with an axe handle, pistol, sap, and several knives.

Feeling like sacrificial lambs, the operatives drove in silence as they listened to Joby recite the rules of play. As "undercover Hells Angels," the operatives could take the Banditos out in a surprise ambush.

"We don't want to tip off the enemy," Joby explained.

Bird's mind raced as Joby rambled on about the Grand Plan to execute "those motherfuckers." Bird caught Timmy's pained expression through the rearview mirror. Sweat slicked his head and his breath was shallow. Pops was the color of stone and sat motionless in the back seat, a far away look in his eyes. *Shit,* Bird panicked. There was no chance to warn Beef about the pending slaughter. Bird watched the fuel gauge nervously. Full tank. *Shit. Pull over,* he telegraphed, his mind racing. The road stretched before them like a long scream, but they were approaching a small town. Five miles.

"We should fuel up here," Bird swallowed, pointing to the gas gauge, "there won't be another pump for miles." *Please please please,* he could hear his own breath, as if he were underwater and using a snorkel.

Joby shrugged, looked at his gas gauge, and pulled over.

"I'll just top it off," he said.

"I'm going to use the restroom," Bird pointed to the back of the station, his heart pounding. *Please be a phone there,* he pleaded. He needed to contact Beef now. "Here's the deal," Bird cradled the pay phone to his ear, keeping one eye on the gas pumps and the other on the restroom, "we've been ordered to kill Banditos. Get every cop you can on line in Vegas and make sure you tell them to stop, arrest, harass, do whatever the fuck they have to do to keep the Banditos away from the Eagles Lodge."

The conversation took less than two minutes. Bird had to trust that Beef would make the phone calls and rally the necessary forces. He had to believe his efforts would thwart a major bloody confrontation. As he climbed back into the Jeep, he gave Timmy and Pops a hard stare.

Around six that afternoon the operatives arrived at the Eagles Lodge in Las Vegas. The army of Hells Angles was a gathering of misfits, freakish looking soldiers without uniforms. They grunted greetings to each other and grim-faced staked out their respective positions in the parking lot, across the street, inside the bar, waiting in an eerie half-light for the enemy.

As Bird and Timmy dutifully crouched behind a parked car, Bird felt his chest constrict. For the first time during the investigation, he felt truly helpless. His two-minute phone call to Beef was his only link to the outside and to possible relief. He jumped at the sound of a car backfiring, a horn honking, a tire squealing. Boots crunching over gravel unnerved him. He could hear Timmy's teeth click.

Bird swallowed, a metallic taste in his mouth. He had chewed the insides of his cheeks until they bled. Bird imagined this was how soldiers must feel in combat, waiting breathless in trenches for the battle to start. Their focus so intense that sounds amplified, colors brightened, and smells startled the senses. Bird barely breathed as he waited, dizzy with anticipation, painfully aware that he was playing Russian roulette and the gun was pointed at his head. They were outnumbered and would absolutely die if the three of them confronted the Hells Angels.

Mercifully, no Banditos arrived.

By 8:00 P.M. the Hells Angels called it a night, shook hands with each other, exchanged warm hugs, and thanked each other for their support.

Bird and Timmy exchanged looks of stunned disbelief. Timmy was sweating so much he looked as if he had fallen into a swimming pool. Bird breathed for the first time in several minutes and felt the blood return to his head. He wanted to quit, *fuck this investigation, fuck all of you,* he shuddered, regaining his composure. He might have survived round one, but Bird knew the Russian roulette was far from over.

Joby slapped Bird on the back, shoved his shotgun into Bird's hands, and ordered him to "hold it for him" in case law enforcement stopped him. "They know me around here," Joby explained. "I'm not going to prison for this." They departed in separate cars, but not ten minutes later, Joby stopped at a gas station off Interstate 515, waved over the operatives, and introduced them to Phil, the Hells Angels "West Coast hook" for firearms and explosives. Phil advised them that he had suppliers for hand grenades, silencers, and remote-controlled bombs. He scribbled his phone number on the back of his business card and winked at Bird, "For you, anything."

By the time the operatives reconvened at the Skull Valley clubhouse, it was midnight and Galliano greeted them warmly, called them his "soldiers."

"Sorry for the false alarm," he apologized, alluding to the shoot-out that never occurred. "Sometimes we have to chase ghosts to defend our territory and reputation."

Ghosts—the invisible enemy—the Banditos.

CHASING GHOSTS

Ironically, "chasing ghosts" boosted the status of the operatives in the eyes of the Hells Angels. They proved that they were willing to die for the Hells Angels to further the Cause.

And the payoff was big.

The Hells Angels trusted the operatives with their weapons and authorized them to traffic arms and drugs across the border for profit. As a general rule, prospects were prohibited from carrying guns, but Dusty, in uncharacteristic fashion, loaned Bird his Taurus .357 revolver to hold during Skull Valley church meetings. Joby solicited Bird for arms deals and asked him to sell his Browning .270 semiautomatic rifle to "contacts in Mexico." Bird made it a point never to be greedy. The rules were simple: the Hells Angels supplied the guns, and Bird trafficked them to Mexico and sold the weapons on the Mexican black market for a 500 percent markup. Bird had played his part well, splitting his fake profits with the club, making huge donations to the charter "just because," and making it appear that he was getting rich.

Not only did the Hells Angels believe the operatives could broker deals for them south of the border, but they sanctioned arms transactions in Vegas with Phil as well. The Hells Angels willingly gave the operatives freedom to travel, guns to broker, and cash to trade—all solid evidence in the case against them. The Skull Valley charter's treatment of the operatives sparked jealous rivalry among other club members. Bird and his team weren't like "other" prospects, doing grunt work and "making their bones." They held a different status—they made money for the Hells Angels.

Two days later, while traveling through Bullhead City on their way to meet Phil in Las Vegas and broker another arms transaction, Bird fielded phone calls from Smitty, who advised that he was "keeping tabs on the operatives" because he predicted soon they would be "movie stars," rewarded for their great performances. Besides, Smitty added, he wanted to "assist" with Silent Steve's business—murder for hire—and knew of a Hells Angel in San Francisco who had done contract hits before. Smitty wanted to know Bird's opinion.

His *opinion*? Bird smothered a smile. Smitty wasn't interested in helping Silent Steve. He was baiting Bird.

Something curious was happening. Hells Angels were vying for Bird's attention, flattering him—"movie star"—soliciting his advice on murder. Unwittingly, Bird had become the "go-to" guy for criminal activity, and he wasn't yet a full-patched Hells Angel. He couldn't lie—part of him enjoyed this attention, this crazy worship from a group of sickly deviant people, not because it milked his ego, but because it validated his purpose. Black Biscuit's purpose.

Beef had grown restless with the operatives over the last few weeks, no doubt pressured from ATF brass. The battery of questions continued to be the same: Was it really necessary to go deeper? Didn't they have enough evidence to convict these guys? Each day the operatives lived among the Hells Angels only increased their risk of death. Case in point, the planned ambush of the Banditos. The operatives had become pawns in the sick game of Russian roulette.

The game continued.

"This is over," Beef insisted.

"We're too close," Bird argued. "We can do this."

Bird knew that as long as they kept producing evidence, they could pacify the brass. But Bird also knew that they had to continue to speed up the prospecting process. The operatives had already earned the Hells Angels trust and respect following the Bandito affair, but Bird knew the operatives couldn't survive another "ghost-chasing" mission or direct orders to kill. At some point their luck would run out.

Bird and Timmy arrived in Las Vegas shortly after nine in the evening and arranged to meet with Phil at a popular sports bar. The atmosphere inside the place was festive—in direct contrast to the business the operatives planned to discuss with Phil. A woman in white face paint, with deep red lips, served Bird a beer. Her dress was sequined, low-cut, and missing its back. She flashed her polka-dot panties at Bird, grinned, and turned away.

Other disturbing—almost ethereal—characters floated through the bar, either high or too drunk to mind the voyeurs. Bird felt a strange kind of calm as he people-watched, realizing for the first time in many months that he wasn't the freak show, that he was finally ordinary and could enjoy a beer at a bar and not field reproachful stares. He had lived so long in costume that sometimes he forgot what he looked like to other people. It felt good to be inconspicuous.

At the bar a she-man with a handsome chiseled face placed her large hand over Timmy's and asked him for his phone number. "Fucking freak," Timmy mumbled and shooed his "admirer" away.

As if on cue, Phil arrived. He was a young, muscular biker, with no neck, who resembled a toad. His small eyes were skittish as he met Bird's stare and slipped him a note on a note pad that read, "Charter Funding."

Phil thrust his tongue into his upper lip and without a word pointed to the written list:

- Uzi $1,700
- Colt $1,100 with tube (silencer)
- 2 eggs (hand grenades) $1,000 each
- Shotgun $500
- Mac-11 $600

Phil was a middleman, his source was a character named "Bobby" who worked for him at Charter Funding. Bobby was "dialed in" in Las Vegas and had the ability to build remote-controlled explosive devices powerful enough to "take down a whole building." Phil pulled out a pen and paper and instructed Bird to "write down" his wish list on a cocktail napkin.

Bird obliged and placed his order:

- AR-15 silencer
- Uzi with silencer
- Eggs
- C-4
- Remote-controlled bombs

At the very least Bird could remove a few more illegal weapons from the streets and build clout with the Skull Valley group until he could devise a plan to move the operatives forward faster.

"Bobby will have these items to you in two weeks," Phil grunted and pocketed the napkin. "The bombs will be disguised as other items, like a briefcase."

The exchange with Phil was short, to the point, no nonsense. It didn't matter that Bird had traveled hours to arrange this deal or that he would have to turn around in minutes and return to the Skull Valley clubhouse for debriefing. Never mind that the operatives also had to squeeze in a meeting with Beef to report updates and log evidence. It was a nightly, exhausting ritual but a necessary chore.

As prospects Timmy and Bird served the whims of their sponsors; punctuality was strictly monitored and enforced. If they were no-shows to a scheduled event, or simply late, they would have to field questions, fill in gaps, and explain their apparently misguided priorities. If they wanted to be Hells Angels, they would make sure they did everything in their power to serve the members, to die for the club, and pledge their loyalty to the gangster lifestyle.

There was no room for error.

That Black Biscuit's headquarters, located in Tempe, and the Hells Angels clubhouse, situated in Prescott, posed logistical complications, was of little significance. The operatives were expected to serve two masters at once, and neither side really cared how that feat was accomplished, only that it was done. The motorcycle trailer saved precious minutes, but that option continued to be risky. Bird worried about impromptu traffic stops, breakdowns, and driver incompetence. There was no time to get lost.

Bird took a long pull on his beer as he marshaled what energy he had left to return to Skull Valley and then push on to Williams, Arizona, just two hours from the Grand Canyon and nearly six from Las Vegas. The operatives were expected to sell support T-shirts and guard Skull Valley officers at an Arizona motorcycle rally. Bird asked the white-faced waitress for the time: 9:30 P.M. If they hustled, they could still make their date by eleven the next morning.

The pace was not only exhausting for the operatives, but it also proved to be a logistical nightmare for the surveillance crew. There was no such thing as an itinerary. As a general rule prospects were supplied information on an "as needed basis." Locations changed rapidly, plans deviated, and deals fell through unexpectedly. Spontaneity was the norm. Bird and his team needed to be prepared to switch gears at a moment's notice. Without crank to fuel sleep-deprived and nutritionally depleted bodies, Bird and his team had trouble maintaining the pace of endless partying. And the suits grew frustrated, complaining of explosive egos and things not going according to plan.

The chasm between Suits and Streets widened.

ATF brass couldn't comprehend the sudden shifts in activities or the value in—not to mention funding of—agents who stood around for hours and hours in hot sun waiting to take the next hot dog order. Pressure on the operatives mounted as well as they struggled to deliver intelligence, firm up transactions, and gather evidence to justify their continued infiltration.

It was nine thirty in the evening and Bird was already drained. He closed his eyes: the image of Beef fuming was to his left; he saw his team "hammering" off to his right; and there, over the top of his head was Dusty, grinning. Bird's head hurt.

"Prospect!" Timmy parroted, tapping his beer stein into Bird's bottle. "It's time to move."

Unfortunately, Timmy was right. The prospects were expected to be at the Hog rally the next morning. And so, they spent the rest of that night traveling on a moonlit highway in the back of a surveillance trailer, their heads bouncing against the chrome of their motorcycles.

"We're shutting this down," Beef informed them later at headquarters. "We've got enough on these guys. You're in. You've done it. Mission accomplished."

But Bird still wanted that brass ring—the one thing that would really stick it to these guys—membership. He couldn't deny the investigation was slowing down or that as prospects they'd spent the majority of their time hustling to please members and performing menial tasks that sometimes proved fruitful and other times useless. ATF wanted justification, a reason to continue. Bird knew that if the mission was to survive, he needed to do something dramatic, something over the top to propel the operatives to full-patched status soon. They couldn't wait a full year to go through the motions.

Pops—whose strength always had been in question—was sick, worn out, and trembled as if in shock. Who knew how much longer the old CI could last without compromising the entire investigation. Bird and Beef whispered as much behind his back at meetings. Everyone noticed the spaced out expression in Pops's eyes as if he had passed on already and merely inhabited a physical shell. And there was the danger of his snapping altogether, turning on the operatives out of sheer exhaustion.

It was time to remove Pops.

THE "GIRL" IN MEXICO

JUNE 2003
Pulling Pops out wouldn't be so easy. There had to be a plan or they would all be killed.

"If I have to fetch one more fucking hot dog, . . . " Timmy complained as he jogged back and forth between tents and vendors at the Hog rally, carrying food wrapped in napkins. Bright sun beat down on all of them. Sweat stung their eyes. Bird's legs ached from standing guard. He swatted another fly. After much bickering at headquarters the night before, Bird had convinced Beef to let him try one last ruse. "It'll be our final curtain bow," Bird offered as the operatives and Beef argued around the warehouse table over pots of black coffee and beer nuts. Tension crackled between them. Director and cast were barely speaking—Beef insisted funding was tight, the operation was over, and his ass was on the line. Bird needed more time.

"What if we cast the Hells Angels in lead roles in our play?" Bird began.

"They're already convinced we'd kill for the club," Timmy added.

"What if we did exactly that, killed." Bird spoke slowly, mulling over each thought.

"We'd be instant patches," Timmy insisted.

Beef steamed, his face flush with anxiety as he tapped his pencil on the table. How was he going to sell that to the brass?

"What if we faked a murder but made it look real?" Bird recovered. "I could use my Mexico connections and tell them my scouts have spotted a Mongol wandering around in Magdalena talking shit about the Hells Angels. We could send Pops down to investigate and locate the Mongol," Bird explained. "Then, I'd insist on joining him and bringing an arsenal of guns with me, including a murder weapon. It would give us a chance to disappear for a few days, remove Pops safely, and return as heroes."

"They'll want to see a body," Beef interjected.

"We could recruit a homicide detective from Phoenix PD, have him create a mock murder scene, dress him up in a Mongol vest, pour cow's blood over parts of him, and snap enough photos of the crime scene to be convincing," Bird insisted.

Of course it would work. Bird already had credibility with the club. He was already living the life of a Hells Angel, "ridin' high and livin' free," according to Sonny Barger's motto. The bikers *loved* Bird. Smitty touted him as a "movie star." The Hells Angels would buy Bird's story about a Mongol visiting cantinas in Magdalena. They believed his other story, that he was hauling tractor-trailer loads of guns and bombs into Mexico for huge profits. He had shown pictures to the members—Bird posing with bandito-looking gangsters, all holding M-60s, smiles and arms wrapped around each other with a five-ton load of weed as a backdrop.

Mexico was "open territory"; unclaimed boundaries posed a threat to the Hells Angles. As a now ex-member of the Solo Angeles, the only Mexican club the Hells Angels respected, Bird was regarded as the "white-boy owner of Mexico." Bird had made a point of expressing his repeated gratitude to the Hells Angels for allowing his club to exist in Arizona. Now, his debt was due. If Bird thought a Mongol in Magdalena was a problem, then the Hells Angels would accept it was a problem and Bird's obligation to solve it. Bird had played his role well over the last several months, using his assumed authority on "the Mexico situation" as leverage; he had warned the Hells Angels that the Mongols might use Mexico as a staging point for an attack on or invasion of Arizona.

The wandering Mongol ruse was only the beginning.

But it wasn't enough to have just a Mongol sighting. Bird would need to embellish his story and warn the Hells Angels that his "scouts" had overheard the Mongol disrespecting the club. "He claims you guys were pussies after the Harrah's Casino shootout," Bird would say to incite the bikers. "He's bragged to his Mongol brothers that the Black and White is going to take over the west. They plan to run their meth north through Nogales and into Arizona."

Hells Angel territory.

Silent Steve approached Bird and interrupted his plotting. The biker tore a bite of his hot dog, his eyes like chips, veined and scratchy as if dried too long in the sun. "I definitely want you to take care of that piece of shit we talked about," he swallowed thoughtfully, referring to his earlier proposition to kill his son's murderer. "Make it look like a drug deal gone bad," Silent Steve plotted aloud. "Maybe you can arrange it so that he doesn't show up again at all, you know what I mean? Like a missing person or something."

"Murder is pretty serious," Bird cautioned. "It should be a last resort."

"I know what I want to do. I just can't do it myself," Silent Steve was adamant as he waved his hot dog bun in Bird's face. "I'll bring you a photo and address." He popped the last of his hot dog into his mouth, dropped the bread on the ground, and walked away.

"I appreciate what you're trying to do man," Smitty, who was standing nearby, interjected. "But there's no way any of us can kill this guy. The cops would suspect us first," he paused and said quietly, "I know you can handle this for us. We just need to close this shit up. I miss the old Steve."

Bird swatted another fly and didn't respond.

Smitty patted him on the shoulder and smiled sardonically, "It's your deal man. We're counting on you."

It was perfect.

The Hells Angels already expected Bird to kill for the club. It would only be a matter of time before Silent Steve hounded him for details, wanted updates or trophies from the revenge murder, or worse, grew suspicious about why the man was still alive. Bird had deflected other murders for hire, but this time was different. This time he was a Hells Angel prospect, someone who had pledged to do *anything* for his "brothers," including murder. If he didn't do what Silent Steve expected of him, Bird was fairly certain the biker would make sure Bird "went missing."

But if he distracted the bikers, and planted his Mongol seed, . . .

Bird watched Silent Steve blend back into the crowd and sought out Joby. As expected, Joby was swilling beer with the other Skull Valley officers. Bird took a deep breath. It was now or never.

"My buddies are telling me about a girl in Mexico running his mouth, talking dirt about the Hells Angels," Bird crafted his story. Joby placed his beer down slowly absorbing the news as much as his drunken self could. "Mexico is my responsibility," Bird continued getting bolder. He had bragged that his "Mexico connections" were building "safe houses" for the Hells Angels to hide from the law, live cheaply, and enjoy women, booze, drugs, and warm beaches. It was the "least he could do for the club."

"This Mongol is my problem," Bird emphasized.

Dirty Dan, who stood nearby, was ecstatic, thrilled that the Hells Angels would once again be an intimidating force in Arizona. Dirty Dan offered his advice about killing the Mongol—"You should stab him in the head," or "Fuck him in the ass for a while before you kill him," and be sure to use "thick rubber gloves before shooting. DNA can be traced from guns."

By now Butcher's curiosity was piqued and he piped in enthusiastically, "Fuck him up . . . well let me check with Galliano first."

"I'd go with you, but I got to take the mechanical bull out on a rodeo run," Joby said disappointed.

"Pops will go down first," Bird took his cue.

"Pops?" Joby frowned.

"He's my go-to guy," Bird interjected.

Joby chuckled, "You want to send a ninety-year-old prospect to hunt a Mongol? Shit, if he doesn't get his patch, at least he'll die trying."

"We're just fucking with him," Butcher teased.

"Pops needs this."

"Maybe he's holding on too tight," Butcher said, his eyes darkening.

"If he's not going to make it, . . ." Bird began.

"He'll make it," Butcher said, "you'll all make it. Everyone brags on you guys. Everyone says we stole you. I'll talk to Galliano. I'll have him say something good."

Bird was incredulous. "Good like, 'This McDonald's milkshake is nice and creamy good? As long as I don't forget the fucking capricolla cheese for sandwiches at this week's church good?' We are trying to take out the enemy for the Hells Angels and all we are going to get out of Galliano is some New York, East Coast, old-school bullshit lecture."

Galliano approved of Bird's plan.

Relief smoothed the worry lines on Pops's anxious face as he shook hands with the operatives for the last time. Few words were exchanged though there was an undercurrent of silent gratitude. Pops had been an asset, a wonder, integral to the investigation. And yet he was a criminal, a felon, a liability. Bird could only hope that Pops viewed Black Biscuit as his final chance at redemption, but there was always the specter of betrayal. Sure Pops received a benefit for his efforts, a reduced prison sentence, but he had suffered and he was mentally unstable. He would always pose a risk to the safety of the operatives.

Bird waited a day before breaking the news to the Skull Valley charter. "Pops found the girl in Zacatecas, Mexico," Bird informed Joby at his residence. "I'm headed down there with Timmy. I can't bring a murder weapon back into the United States. Do you have any guns you'd like to sell down there?"

Joby motioned for Bird to follow him into his bedroom where he retrieved a .380 9mm semiautomatic pistol with an obliterated serial number. "She's loaded and ready to fire," Joby advised. "Toss it afterwards," he cautioned, "and be sure to wipe down any fingerprints. I'll tell the boys you're on your way. Let us know what's going on."

"Zacatecas isn't our area," Bird reminded Joby. "We don't know it down there too well. It may take some time. This is central Mexico. We'll just have to see how it goes." He needed to buy time to set the murder stage. Joby hugged Bird as if he were a soldier heading off to war.

"I want you guys to come home. I've been there. I know what it's like. I was involved in the Harrah's casino shootout," Joby said, his voice cracking with emotion.

"I know. You were a warrior," Bird affirmed, appealing again to Joby's ego and hoping he had erased all sarcasm from his voice.

CURTAIN CALL

JUNE 2003

The Phoenix Police Department scrambled to stage the Mongol murder. They selected a dirty patch of Phoenix desert, recruited a Phoenix homicide detective (whom they named "Woody") to play the role of the dead Mongol, smeared cow's blood on the Mongol vest the detective wore, and strategically placed the cow's stomach on the victim's head to resemble a bloody gunshot wound. The detective looked, for all intents and purposes, like a dead Mongol tossed in a ditch with his hands wrapped together with duct tape.

Bird waited until 2:00 A.M. to leave his voice message on Butcher's telephone: "Pops has been shot," Bird lied, hoping his message would incite panic. The murder ruse provided a perfect escape for Pops who, days before, had been safely extricated from the operation and given government protection. Meanwhile, Bird and Timmy perpetuated the murder ruse from the safety of an ATF office. They placed calls to the Hells Angels using their cell phones while they pretended to hunt for Mongols in Mexico.

As Bird expected, news of Pops's predicament sparked a flurry of panicked phone calls to JJ from Skull Valley members and their wives hungry for updates and concerned for JJ's welfare. JJ listened in the darkness of the undercover trailer to the voice messages left at 3:00 A.M., 3:15 A.M., and 3:20 A.M., and a tiny smile curved her lips.

"Any news? Have you heard from Bird? It's not like him to not check in. How long does it take to get to Zacatecas anyway?"

Another day passed.

Bird played on Hells Angels anxiety. He waited until 7:30 P.M. the following day to leave Butcher another cryptic message: "Pops is gone. The Mongol blew a head gasket. The girl is not running anymore." He spoke in code—girl ("Mongol"), gone ("dead"), head gasket ("shot in the head")—mindful that if he were really in Mexico as the Hells Angels believed, he would be worried for his own safety and unable to speak freely.

Meanwhile, Bird arranged to have a FedEx package mailed to JJ from Mexico by an ATF agent so that the box would have a foreign postmark. JJ stayed at the undercover residence and fielded panicked calls from the Hells Angels. She saw Butcher's phone number flash on her caller ID. It was 8:00 P.M. "I need you to come up to the clubhouse, something's happened." His voice was tight.

"Something happened?" JJ pretended.

"Have you heard from Bird?"

"You're fucking freaking me out Butcher," JJ played into his fear. "What do you know that I don't know?" She waited a beat and then said, "Bird sent me a FedEx package from Mexico. I'm not opening it."

Later that night, Bird called Butcher and explained: "Pops got smoked. Timmy and I are trying to get home, but we have to take our time. I can't come racing back across the border after whacking some dude with all the homeland security bullshit. The crossings are hard enough being linked to the club without knowing a body is behind us." In truth, Bird needed to buy time to insert Pops into the witness protection program and to stage the Mongol murder, replete with photographs.

Bird heard heavy breathing. Good, panic had set in.

"Yeah, okay."

"We'll be back in a few days. Tell JJ what's going on. I'm hanging up now."

Butcher summoned the officers. Dusty, who had been Pops's official sponsor, dissolved into tears, raspy heaving sobs, shockingly grief stricken over the loss of his prospect. The Hells Angels were flustered, unsure suddenly how to handle news of Pops's death and his sacrifice for the Hells Angels.

"I heard from Bird. Pops is dead." JJ said the following afternoon. She was quiet waiting for Butcher's reaction. It was 4:00 P.M.

"Don't . . . We need to get this out on the wire. We need to hear the details from Bird."

"I understand," JJ said, reading between the lines. For a brief moment Butcher's invincibility was shattered. He was no longer the "warrior" able to shoot up enemies and return a hero. Pops's death was so unexpected, so . . . unlike a Hells Angel. Butcher was practically speechless. JJ smiled in the darkness of her undercover house. They had pulled it off, the most outrageous of all stunts—they had convinced the Hells Angels that they had actually committed a murder.

At their undercover trailer on a hot June evening two days later, Timmy and Bird fingered the loose threads of the FedEx package that had been sent to JJ. It was 9:00 P.M. Officers of the Skull Valley charter would be arriving soon. Butcher had already warned Bird that the charter wanted to keep news of Pops's death quiet for security reasons. He said that Pops had died "like a true Hells Angel" in reverence and humility and he would later be honored in memoriam. They all would.

Bird stared across the table at his partner, a quiet tension clouding Timmy's eyes. "Why so mopey? We're *Kool and the Gang, easy like Sunday morning* . . . It's patch time," Timmy bluffed, his voice cracking with nerves.

"They might come in here and whack us," Bird warned.

Timmy didn't respond.

There was a knock at the door.

Bird stabbed his cigarette out on the table and tried to stop his legs from shaking. When Butcher and Galliano arrived at the trailer and ordered that everyone inside toss their cell phones into the bushes, Bird wasn't sure whether this would be his final exit. Was he the deer snared in a hunter's trap or were they? Would Joby have second thoughts about having provided Bird with the murder weapon? Would Dusty unleash his anger at having lost Pops on Bird for being foolish enough to send the old salt into battle? Would Galliano, who never approved of anything openly, suddenly put a bullet in Bird's head for having exposed the Hells Angels to police scrutiny?

As the bikers surrounded the table, Butcher's eyes watered. Galliano's jaw twitched. Bird's fingers trembled as he tore open the package and removed the bloody Mongol vest. And just like that, for the first time since the operation began, Bird felt like he had truly won. The members were speechless, choked up, shocked. Bird had done the unthinkable—not only had he killed for the club, but he had killed a Mongol.

"I have pictures too," Bird said and slid the grainy prints across the table. The photos depicted the undercover detective's head, split and bloody, his hands duct taped, his contorted body twisted face down in a shallow grave underneath a Mesquite tree, his Mongol vest plainly visible.

Bird lit a cigarette, his hands shaking. His eyes wet. "Pops got into it with the Mongol in a cantina in Zacatecas, told him that Hells Angels fuck Mongols in the ass for fun. Pops pulled a knife on him and the Mongol shot him twice in the chest."

"We tracked the girl down at a roadside shithole. The fucker left his motorcycle parked in front of his room," Timmy continued, relishing his fifteen minutes of fame.

"We knocked and moved to the side like the police do in the movies because we thought the dude might try to shotgun us through the door. But instead he answered with a fucking fish taco in his hand," Bird completed the story.

"I busted his head open with my ball bat. It sounded like I hit a pumpkin. We took his good-as-dead-soon-to-be-shot Mongol ass out to the desert and taped his hands and feet before we put him in the car. Timmy popped his head open with Joby's .380." Bird waited a beat.

The space was too quiet. He studied the three Hells Angels gathered around the table inside the trailer, his fingers curled around the gun he'd shoved under his leg.

"Sonny knows about the Mongol killing and Pops's death," Galliano said, his eyes welling with emotion. "He wants a personal sit down with you at the USA National Run. He's real proud of you guys."

Galliano grabbed Bird, hugged him, and said, "You did what you had to do. How does it feel to be a Hells Angel?"

Hell's Angel. Bird's head spun. He was in. This was it. The whole operation came down to this moment: the Mongol murder. His heart raced. He tried to contain his excitement.

"We need to get rid of the evidence," Joby said quickly. He removed the digital photograph, floppy computer disk, vest, and FedEx shipping package from the trailer and stashed it in his truck.

"My life and freedom are in that box," Bird cautioned.

"You can trust me brother," Joby said, placing his hand over his heart.

"We'll frame Pops's cut and hang it in the clubhouse," Butcher said. "He gets his patch too. He earned it."

Meanwhile, Dusty was inconsolable. Big Tough Guy Hells Angel in tears over the loss of his prospect. Who knew he was so attached to another human being? That he actually had feelings? Oddly, Dusty had found a kindred spirit in Pops, someone who was as reckless and edgy as he, someone who understood the lure of drugs.

"What about your clothes?" Butcher asked after a while.

"We burned them at the scene," Bird supplied. "Timmy was upset because I forced him to burn a new pair of Red Wing boots," he added for authenticity.

"Spoken like a true Hells Angel," Butcher grinned.

As the members filed out of the trailer to celebrate their victory at the nearest bar, Bird and Timmy stayed behind, promising to join them in a few minutes. The door closed. Bikes roared out of the driveway. Timmy and Bird stood at the table, unmoving. Bird braced himself with his hands and lowered his head. He could barely breathe. The linoleum floor formed dizzy patterns. Suddenly, Timmy snorted, a strange choked laughter filled his lungs as came around the table and grabbed Bird in a bear hug. Tears streamed down his face. "We did it! We made it. We're Hells Angels. We are fucking real Hells Angels. We're there motherfucker!" He whooped releasing Bird from his grip.

Bird smiled weakly. He felt drained as he stumbled toward the living room and slumped on the couch. He was spent, exhausted, mentally, physically, and spiritually. His legs shook from the strain of it all. His hands trembled in his lap and his heart beat alarmingly fast. He wanted to go home, crawl into bed, and draw the blinds. He wanted to live as a bat lives, in darkness.

But he couldn't quite disappear yet. He still had loose ends. He was a "fucking Hells Angel." He should have felt exhilarated even vindicated. This was more than he could ever have imagined.

And yet he felt drained, as if a part of him had died. He had earned the role of a lifetime, and yet he knew he would have to turn it down.

THE RAT

JUNE 2003
Thirty minutes later, Bird stumbled dizzily into the low-level strip club known as the Pinion Pines Bar, owned by Galliano and Butcher. He wasn't in the mood for cheap talent, naked writhing bodies, or beer sprayed in his face. The end of the investigation was bitter sweet. He felt like an actor who had just given his final performance, awed that he had pulled it off, proud of his skills, but also a little depressed. After sacrificing everything "for the good of the cause," he felt almost cheated. His life, his talents lay in the Case. What would it be like to leave the theater and return to his Life? And what kind of career would he have after taking down the Hells Angels?

The Pinion Pines Bar pulsed with primitive erotica, heavy drum beats that matched Bird's heart. Amidst the cheers, sprays of beer, and congratulatory back slaps, Bird was overwhelmed by a pall of apprehension, a strange cloudiness in the bar that made the hair on the back of his neck prick. Butcher eyed him carefully as he downed his beer and said after a moment, "Let's go outside for a minute."

Bird paused, his beer in midair, and caught the glint of something feral in Butcher's expression. *Now what? Had this all been a set up? Was he about to get smoked in the parking lot of this shithole strip club?*

"What's up?" he asked.

Butcher motioned with his head for them to meet outside. Bird never lost eye contact with the biker. "Turn your phone off and leave it in the bed of the pickup truck," Butcher instructed, his eyes shifty, nervous. Air whooshed out of Bird's lungs. He knew what was coming—a confession. No Hells Angel wanted to incriminate himself with recording devices present.

"We have something in common," he began, leaning against his pickup truck. "I also killed someone for the club. You're going to be all spun out for a while. I know you killed dudes before, but when you do it for the club, it's different." He paused, watching Bird's face for reaction.

"Mine was weird. This guy was a rat. They nicknamed me the 'Rat Hunter'," he chuckled. Bird felt suddenly dizzy. Had Butcher suspected him of being a rat? Hot wind blew against his cheeks. They were alone in the parking lot. Not a car on the street. No back up. Just the loud beat of rock filled the space between them.

"This rat was responsible for putting a bunch of Hells Angels in prison," Butcher continued matter-of-factly, folding his arms across his chest. Bird's mouth was parched. He needed moisture desperately. Timmy was still inside. Alone. Maybe he'd realize Bird was missing?

"I'm telling you this because it took me five months to get my 'Filthy Few' patch. I had to wait. We may have to wait to officially patch you guys. You're in; you're members and all. You're going to be treated like members. You may just have to wait to get your patches."

Bird couldn't believe what he was hearing. They had to wait to get their patches? He couldn't wait. He was done. They needed to raid the club-houses now, get the investigation before a grand jury. Wait? Anger simmered inside Bird. "Fuck that," he exploded. "We earned them. All the talk about 'do the right thing,' 'being old school,' 'this is how we do shit back east.' We did all that. We acted old school. We took out a Mongol. Pops got killed and we want the cloth."

"It may not be that easy," Butcher soothed.

Disgusted, Bird walked back inside the bar and directly up to Joby. "What the fuck is going on? What is this wait shit?"

"I'm going to sell your case to the west coast officers. We need their okay," Joby explained. "You can have my patch if they make you wait.

"I didn't wait for anyone to say okay before I fucking killed that Mongol." Bird was defensive.

"The problem is the law is going to know that you did some dirt to get your patches so quick. They start looking at you, then they start looking at us. They look at us; they look at the Hells Angels. They look at the Hells Angels and that's not good."

"Let 'em look, Joby," Bird protested. "They ain't gonna see anything. What they need is a thousand miles deep in Mexico and probably scattered around the desert by the coyotes by now." Bird was hot.

"We need to ditch the vest." Joby sat and motioned for Bird and Timmy to follow him. He led them back to the clubhouse where he methodically put on leather gardener's gloves and removed a pair of scissors from his back pocket.

"DNA gentlemen," he quipped and began to cut the bloodied Mongol vest into strips. He collected the cloth piles and put them in a bag. "I've got a spot to show you," he said.

It was dark. Moonless. Joby gave directions as Timmy drove and Bird lay in the back seat watching the black sky rush past him. His mind raced. They were alone in the car with a Hells Angel enforcer on a road that snaked through rugged mountains. There were no road signs, no guideposts, no way for anyone to follow them. Or find them. There was no chance to alert Beef or any of the surveillance crew. No cell phone service. And Bird saw no headlights following. He caught Timmy's anxious gaze through the rearview mirror. Timmy knew something was up too. Two against one. They could take Joby out . . . if they had to. *Fine way to end a case,* Bird grumbled to himself. That's just what he and Timmy needed, ATF Internal Affairs.

But as the miles stretched, Bird sobered. If Joby had meant to kill them, he would have done so by now. Why would he drive nearly 40 miles from the clubhouse just to smoke them?

They arrived shortly after midnight at an old horse pen in the middle of nowhere. Exhausted, Bird opened the truck door and spotted a fifty-five-gallon drum a few yards ahead of him.

Joby lit a match inside the drum and burned each Mongol strip. Bird and Timmy eventually joined in feeling part of a strange funeral for Pops.

They spent the next hour reminiscing about the old CI until finally Bird announced, "Last piece." As he held the bloody strip, he ceremoniously toasted Pops, tossed the evidence into the fire, and said, "Fuck the Mongols and long live the Hells Angels."

"Angels forever, forever Angels," Joby cheered.

Less than three days later, Beef shut down Operation Black Biscuit.

CLOSING CREDITS

JULY 2003

In the weeks before the operatives became full-patched members, Beef had grown increasingly concerned about reported rumors spreading outside the state that the operatives were fakes. Various factions within the Arizona Hells Angels were friendly with members in California, and whether out of jealousy or something more sinister, the bikers began to inquire of Teacher, the Solo Angeles member in California, whether Bird and his team were legitimate outlaws.

Teacher learned from his cohorts in Mexico that Bird and company were never "made" Solo Angeles. Beef knew it was only a matter of time before the rumors reached the Skull Valley chapter and the operatives faced certain execution. Beef wasn't about to take the chance that he could successfully thwart another plot against Bird's life if given sufficient warning. The Chico Affair, as it was later referred, had been too close a call.

The Mongol murder posed an added complication.

The operatives had proved to the Hells Angels that they were bona fide killers. They would be expected to kill again. But more serious was the knowledge that with any killing there had to be repercussion; the Hells Angels would become suspicious if no police investigation ensued, no body was recovered, and no reprisal from the Mongols. Beef knew that a Mongol killing, even a fake one, would likely start a biker war, the ramifications of which, neither he nor his agency was prepared to combat. Unlike the

Mongols, the Hells Angels were the most prolific biker club in the world. They had international members. Never mind the logistical nightmare of monitoring and managing his own personnel, Beef couldn't begin to prepare his agency or his team for the safety problems he would likely encounter with a full-blown biker war. Beef reasoned with the operatives that at some point every actor must exit the stage, end the production, and drop the curtain.

If Beef allowed the operatives to continue as full-patched Hells Angels, he also had to contend with surveillance issues and information leaks. Monitoring a female agent, no less, posed even more hurdles. Each operative had perpetuated his own story. JJ talked with the biker's old ladies and would inevitably be thrown into that mix, separate from her team. The biker culture would never permit a blending of the women with the men. Beef envisioned crazy scenarios in which he would have to secure surveillance just to monitor JJ and the old ladies. And as "fresh bait," JJ might be subjected to certain ritual rites of passage that would not only compromise the investigation but also endanger her.

Unlike other cases where infiltrations involved just one federal agent, Operation Black Biscuit was an enterprise, and Beef was ultimately responsible for the welfare of a team. That burden had become too much for Beef to bear. Never mind that funding had become a monumental problem; surveillance was expensive and required manpower from multiple agencies. The Department of Public Safety, Phoenix Police Department, Glendale Police Department, and Tempe Police Department had all supplied crew members and their patience was waning.

Beef had had enough pacifying wounded egos and bitter squabbles amongst his crew, some of whom never saw the value in solitary sitting for hours on end simply watching and waiting. The hours and hours of boredom punctuated by moments of terror drained the surveillance team, many of whom had left and been replaced, and replaced again, during the course of the investigation.

Plus, the Phoenix Police Department had started to grumble. They wanted to reassign Timmy. But extricating yet another member of the operation would prove fatal. Over Bird's protests, Beef ordered the operatives to disappear and take long-deserved vacations. They had already accomplished more than anyone ever hoped or imagined possible.

No one had ever infiltrated the Hells Angels.

"The goal was never to become full-patched members," Bird explained during his Top Cops interview. "It was to get inside the organization, gather as much intelligence as we could, and find the perpetrators of a murder. Becoming full patched was just the crowning accomplishment, the Holy Grail. We're in their heads. We infiltrated their club. It *can* be done. And it can be done again."

Black Biscuit's headquarters was immediately dissolved, like a Hollywood set, broken down to its original vacant warehouse. Bird's undercover residence was also converted back to an empty house, as if nothing remarkable had occurred there. Bird and his team were reduced to mere ghosts haunting the halls and kitchen of the residence's dark cavelike interior. For safety reasons the operatives didn't dare return to recover their personal articles.

Over the next several months, Beef was instrumental in ensuring that the prosecution of the case progressed. As the case agent for Operation Black Biscuit, Beef orchestrated agency-wide search warrants, authored countless affidavits, assisted in the asset forfeiture and seizure of Hells Angels clubhouses and paraphernalia, and supervised the arrests and eventual indictments of sixteen high-ranking Hells Angels members on charges ranging from murder, murder for hire, violation of RICO laws, and drug trafficking. Most faced possible life prison terms.

During this time law enforcement recovered a frightening arsenal of illegal weapons, more than 650 fully automatic firearms, machine guns, silencers and bombs, and 30,000 rounds of ammunition. The government assembled 800 hours of bugged conversations, 92,000 phone calls, and 8,500 seized documents.

Black Biscuit was all of their legacies—at once an undercover success and a sting operation turned horribly sour. The operatives may have crippled the Hells Angels enterprise, but like a true crime family, the club was self-perpetuating and there would always be replacements.

The threat of reprisals was real. None of the members arrested remained in custody pending trial. One Hells Angel, who allegedly murdered the

Mesa clubhouse woman and is still a fugitive[15] taunted the operatives from an Internet Web site: "Catch me if you can," one note read, with the suspect's photograph attached at myspace.com. "The ladies call me blue eyes . . . I live to ride for the Hells Angels."

BEEF

Three days after the round up, Hells Angels began their intimidation campaign, targeting Beef's family first, showing up unannounced at his front door and threatening the death of his wife and kids.

There were hang-up calls and warnings whispered over Beef's telephone line. Beef installed cameras and security systems and demanded surveillance. But the threats continued. Notice didn't matter and didn't relieve his children's nightmares. Beef had few choices and waiting for the system to extract the members from the streets after trial, maybe a year or two or three down the road, wasn't an acceptable option. Instead, Beef played their game, dialed Mesa Bob directly, and threatened him with reprisal if he didn't call off his hounds. Beef had leverage. After all, it wouldn't do the chapter president much good if the Red and White learned that Mesa Bob was responsible for giving the Solos permission to exist in Arizona.

"You think I'm stupid enough to send guys to a federal agent's house?" Mesa Bob was on the defensive.

"This isn't the circus. I have been doing this for a long time. I told you I have hundreds of hours of recordings. I know what you are doing now. If you think I can't find you, you better think again," Beef replied.

Later, the chapter president would whine to his defense attorney that Beef had threatened him, promised him that he would go to prison for life, and that he had three options: kill himself, cooperate, or take his time like a man. Mesa Bob did none of the three. More hang-up calls followed and visits to the homes of other officers. Internet chat room threats against

---

[15] Hells Angel Kevin Augustiniak's murder charges were dismissed in federal U.S. District Court but revived by the Maricopa County Attorney's Office. Michael Kramer, the other murder suspect, was a key ATF informant who neglected to reveal his role in the crime to agents. He had spent months as a paid operative. Kramer's plea involved no prison time.

the agents continued. And still no support came from the United States Attorney's Office to prosecute old cases against the Hells Angels that could have at least held the bikers in custody and given the agents some reprieve. The cases had been shelved for lack of interest; the drug seizures were too insignificant or the effort to be expended wasn't worth the payoff.

But then the inevitable happened: the Hells Angels put out a contract hit on Bird's life. And ATF acknowledged that maybe the agents weren't so safe and could use some protection. Whether ATF was truly concerned for Bird's welfare or worried about liability, ATF became aggressive, pouncing at the chance to arrest any Hells Angel they could find no matter how small the charge—felon in possession, possession of a single tab of ecstasy, or illegally wearing a bulletproof vest. The game had changed.

"It's the three-for-one rule," Beef taunted as he watched one Hells Angel paraded away in handcuffs in front of twelve of his brothers. "You guys come after one of us, we are coming after three of you. Just taking care of business you little bitch."

As the sixteen Hells Angels awaited trial, their unindicted brothers seethed at reports that their own had been so naive as to allow undercover cops to infiltrate their organization. During their weekly church meetings, over coffee and beer at their clubhouses, they spun the extraneous and meaningless conspiracy theories. Their paranoia and suspicion dissolved their precious protocol: Members talked out of turn, spread vicious rumors against one another, and violated their codes of brotherhood. They made plans to retaliate against their own.

TIMMY

Timmy, after a year of training in another state, returned to his police agency and resumed investigations into other, unrelated, gangs. He lived a subdued existence, haunted by shadows over his shoulder and the specter of testifying against the Hells Angels.

JJ

JJ, meanwhile, relocated to another ATF division and attempted to resume her career, although after working months in deep cover with unlimited autonomy, she found it difficult to conform to ATF protocol and procedure. Every other investigation paled in comparison with Operation Black Biscuit. "Of course I was afraid. I'll always be afraid. If you're not afraid, you're not human," she conceded in her Top Cops interview, "but you go on."

BIRD

Bird didn't disappear. In truth he sensed there would be no hiding place for him or his team, no federal escorts, and no safe houses, and because neither he nor any members of his team was even close to retiring, there would be no easy exit from deep-cover life. Bird felt exposed, like lightening flashed over a field. Not afraid exactly, but anxious, unsure how the case against the Hells Angels would evolve. Or how his family would cope with the repercussions and the certain threats of reprisal. Bird had been involved in other risky operations but none like this, none that left him this breathless. His was a life interrupted. There *was* no follow-up role for him, no climax. It wasn't as if he could resume his career.

Bird had cultivated his fake identity for so many years, he wasn't sure he could stop. Or even wanted to. He had a gorgeous home he rarely occupied. He visited his sanctuary, admired the frog pond with its large flat lilies that resembled dripping hearts. He loved the cold cavelike feel of his adobe living room, with its bumpy clay walls, wide arches, wood-beamed ceiling, and terra-cotta tiles. But a part of him liked the space because he felt buried alive, underground, protected. Maybe subconsciously that was why he preferred his family remain in the home. In truth he knew he would have to sell it; he was in too much danger. The Hells Angels would surely target his family first and punish him where it hurt the most.

When Bird returned home, his children recoiled at his frightening appearance, and his wife wore a veil of sadness. Each knew instinctively that some kind of end was coming. Bird saw it in his wife's expression—the father their children knew, the man she married had forever changed. In the end their relationship would be a casualty of Operation Black Biscuit.

Although his agency did its best to redact his name and conceal his identity from the ensuing media barrage and mountains of defense discovery, Bird knew his secret life was over.

The Hells Angels believed he was a rat.

But ATF rewarded rats, and Bird and his team enjoyed quiet recognition for their efforts, earning Top Cop awards for bravery and courage from the National Association of Police Officers. Bird tucked his award away in a bank vault and slipped back into some kind of life without government protection, bodyguards, or sadly, even at times government interest.

Bird resisted reporting any threats to ATF though he certainly had his share. He knew ATF was hungry to transfer him out of state. The liability was killing them. But Bird wasn't one to run. He wasn't afraid of his accomplishments. And he refused to live his life as a victim. The last thing he wanted was government protection or restrictions on his freedom. He had cases to work, trial testimony and evidence to prepare, a family to restore. He didn't need more turmoil.

But after spending eighteen months working deep cover, in the company of four anxious faces and a crew of dedicated behind-the-scenes producers, Bird did the only thing he knew how to do: he returned to the streets as an understudy, substituting for other agents on an as-needed basis, to assume the role of a dope dealer for small-time narcotics busts. As unglamorous as his parts were, Bird needed to work the streets and was lost at a desk job shuffling papers, investigating cases behind the scenes. He felt warehoused as he accepted various rotations, assisting other agents on their cases and settling into the background of the Hells Angels raids. But he resisted his ATF bosses for only so long before his situation became too dangerous, and he was forced to leave the state.

Three months after the raids began, while Bird was working a new case with a partner, he encountered a Hells Angel, the tattoo artist, Mac, who had inked up Bird's arms at the Rose Tattoo Parlor. Mac was out on bond. Bird was off duty enjoying downtime seated at a bar surrounded by crowds of drinkers. Bird tensed. He tightened his grip on the neck of his beer. Bird should have been used to surprise, but Mac's presence caught him off guard, rattled him. He wasn't prepared to take a bullet.

Dying wasn't part of his plan. He met Mac's gaze and stared him down like an animal cornered. Bird had no surveillance team to rescue him, and his partner hadn't registered the threat. Bird's eyes flicked to Mac's waist—no weapon. Bird relaxed as he realized Mac wasn't about to give him the satisfaction of an easy exit. The Hells Angels were more interested in inflicting terror—real or imagined. *Chasing ghosts.* They wanted to paralyze Bird, make him fear shadows that climbed his stone walls, jump at quiet ripples in his backyard pond, and jolt at the shrill ring of his telephone late at night when his kids and wife slept restlessly in the same room, afraid to turn the lights off or to sleep alone.

"You won't get away with this punk bitch," the biker seethed, his voice a threatening whisper. "We'll find you. We'll get you. For the rest of your life, you'll be running from the devil."

EPILOGUE

No one, no prospect, no member, absolutely no undercover cop, ever rode a motorcycle less and accomplished more in a club investigation than Bird. Not possible.

—Christopher Bayless, ATF special agent, Chicago

U.S. Case vs. The Hells Angels Fizzles
Racketeering Counts Dismissed

—Dennis Wagner, *Arizona Republic*

A much ballyhooed racketeering case against Arizona's Hells Angels Motorcycle Club has all but ended in federal court with the U.S. Attorney's Office dismissing charges against some defendants and settling for lesser convictions against the rest.

The government's case of drug violations, gun running, murder, racketeering and other crimes came to a close Wednesday, in part because of a feud between federal prosecutors and undercover agents with the Bureau of Alcohol, Tobacco, Firearms and Explosives.

The result:

Authorities failed to convict any of the 16 defendants on the key charge of racketeering, or running a criminal enterprise.

Half of those indicted were given plea deals on lesser offenses.

Federal charges against five others were dismissed.

Under the indictment, most of the bikers faced possible life terms.

As a result of plea deals, none [will serve] more than five years in federal prison. The U.S. Attorney's Office described the outcome as a "good thing" because eight defendants pled guilty.

In March 2006, in what was anticipated to be a mega trial lasting sixteen weeks, the case against the remaining Hells Angels abruptly ended, steeped in interagency politics and accusations. Feuds concerning discovery violations threatened the integrity of the evidence and led to heated arguments in the federal judge's chambers between ATF agents and the United States Attorney's Office.

But in the end no amount of political or legal jousting could upstage what really happened: Operation Black Biscuit served as a dire warning to the Arizona Hells Angels. The club was not invincible, it could be infiltrated, and it could happen again.

★ ★ ★

From Hero to Scapegoat

I am now a man without a country. I am up against the crime syndicate that I infiltrated and the agency that abandoned me . . . My family lives in fear.

—Jay Dobyns, *The Arizona Republic*, January 14, 2007

In May 2006, Jay Dobyns (aka Bird), who is now on leave from ATF and has assumed an alias, filed a multimillion-dollar lawsuit against his agency, claiming his bureau failed to protect him and ignored credible death threats against him and his family. Once hailed on *America's Most Wanted* as one of the "good guys" who brings down the criminals, Dobyns accused his agency, in an eighty-three-page grievance that was submitted to former ATF deputy director Edward Domenech, of multiple acts of "mismanagement, retaliation, harassment, and defamation."

Domenech responded to Dobyns's allegations by stating in his "notice of grievance decision" that if any mistakes were made in the agency's communication with Dobyns about possible death threats, they were "unintentional." As added emphasis, ATF denied Dobyns personal protection, accused him of fraud and of being psychologically unfit for duty, ordered his multiple transfers, and ultimately blocked Dobyns from receiving a Medal of Valor.

Dobyns, who has since sought public support for his plight by appearing on national media broadcasts such as CNN's *Anderson Cooper 360* in January 2007 and local news coverage in *The Arizona Republic*, specifically charged, among other agency abuses, that ATF never disclosed to Dobyns a prison inmate's calculated plan to murder him and torture his daughter. Dobyns explained to Anderson Cooper that his name has circulated amongst prison inmates on a so-called "green-light list" that targeted him for assassination. Dobyns alleged in his lawsuit that ATF was privy to a more recent death threat issued by a Hells Angels member awaiting trial for murder. In jail correspondence to another inmate, the biker described how Dobyns could "end up getting AIDS from a dirty needle and die a slow miserable death . . . [or] he will get a bad dose of steroids, send a blood clot to his brain, have a stroke, and be . . . retarded." Included in the mail were graphic details concerning the torture of Dobyns's wife.

ATF could have moved Dobyns and his family under what is known as a "threat policy," which is similar to the kind of protection the government routinely gives witnesses in organized crime cases. But federal agents who go undercover don't automatically receive a high level of protection.

In Dobyns's case, his agency quibbled over his stated risk level and ultimately made a financial decision: "In order to save money, I was told it wasn't cost effective," Dobyns told Anderson Cooper on CNN. Instead, Dobyns moved himself and his family several times—at his own expense—to elude those who'd threatened to kill him.

In an unprecedented move, Dobyns made the ultimate sacrifice and blew his own cover by announcing to the world in January that he was Jay Dobyns, federal agent, father, husband, and—sadly now—a Hells Angels target. After spending a lifetime quietly accepting accolades and praise for his superb undercover performances as ATF's star, Dobyns is now engaged in the fight of his life—his own.

ACKNOWLEDGMENTS

A special thanks to Sergei for supporting me during the writing of this project despite the many risks and challenges involved.

Thanks to Rob Kirkpatrick, my editor at Lyons Press, for enduring the complications surrounding the writing of this book.

Thanks to Lisa Renee Jones for her faith in me and her constant encouragement and guidance.

Thanks to Robert G. Diforio of the D4EO Literary Agency for his help with the sale and placement of this book.

Many thanks to Jo-Ann Power for her invaluable guidance through this process.

My sincere admiration and thanks to all those sources, who cannot be named, for their important contributions.

APPENDIX: THE FALLEN FEW

Mesa Bob (aka Robert Johnston, Jr.), indicted on one count of Title 18 USC, Section 1962(c) RICO, and Title 18 USC, Section 1962 (d) RICO conspiracy, DISMISSED; pled to Misprision of a Felony, to wit: Possession with Intent to Distribute less than 5 grams of methamphetamine, a Schedule II Controlled Substance, a class E felony with a maximum prison term of three years.

Smitty (aka Donald Smith), indicted on one count of Title 18 USC, Section 1962(c) RICO, and Title 18 USC, Section 1962 (d) RICO conspiracy, DISMISSED.

Chef Boy Are Dee (aka Dennis Denbesten), indicted on one count of Title 18 USC, Section 1962(c) RICO, and Title 18 USC, Section 1962 (d) RICO conspiracy, Dismissed; pled guilty to Possession of a Firearm, a class C Felony, maximum prison term ten years.

Cal (aka Calvin Schaefer), indicted on one count of Title 18 USC, Section 1962(c) RICO, and Title 18 USC, Section 1962 (d) RICO conspiracy, DISMISSED; pled guilty to Possession of a Firearm in furtherance of a drug trafficking crime, a class A felony, maximum sentence, life in prison.

Dee (aka Douglas Dam), indicted on one count of Title 18 USC, Section 1962(c) RICO, and Title 18 USC, Section 1962 (d) RICO conspiracy, DISMISSED.

Galliano (aka Teddy Toth), indicted on Conspiracy to Commit Murder, DISMISSED; pled guilty to obstruction of justice, a class C felony, maximum prison term, twenty years.

Mac (aka Robert McKay), indicted on assault with individual counts of Title 18 USC, Section 1959(a)(1); pled guilty to Intimidating a Federal Officer, class A misdemeanor, time served.

Dusty (aka Rudy Jaime), indicted on one count of Title 18 USC, Section 1962(c) RICO, and Title 18 USC, Section 1962 (d) RICO conspiracy, DISMISSED; pled guilty to Possession with Intent to Distribute 50 grams of methamphetamine a class D felony, with a maximum term of twenty years in prison.

Hank (aka Henry Watkins), indicted on one count of Title 18 USC, Section 1962(c) RICO, and Title 18 USC, Section 1962 (d) RICO conspiracy, DISMISSED.

Butcher (aka Robert Rienstra), indicted on Conspiracy to Commit Murder, DISMISSED.

Joby (aka George Walters), indicted on one count of Title 18 USC, Section 1962(c) RICO, and Title 18 USC, Section 1962 (d) RICO conspiracy, DISMISSED.

Fang (aka Craig Kelly), indicted on Title 18 USC, section 922 (g)(1) and (924(a)(2), Conspiracy and Assault, DISMISSED.

Rod (aka Elton Ward), pled guilty to Intent to Distribute less than 5 grams of Methamphetamine, a class B felony, with a maximum prison term of forty years.

Animal (aka Andrew Murphy), indicted on one count of Title 18 USC, Section 1962(c) RICO, and Title 18 USC, Section 1962 (d) RICO conspiracy, DISMISSED; pled guilty to Possession with Intent to Distribute 50 grams of methamphetamine, a class C felony, with a maximum prison term of twenty years.

Michael Kramer, pled guilty to racketeering, no prison time ordered.

Kevin Augustiniak, indicted on murder charges, DISMISSED, but refiled by the Maricopa County Attorney's Office and pending trial.

Paul Eischied, indicted on murder charges, pending his capture.

INDEX